COLLEGE SUCCESS GUARANTEED 2.0

Other Title by the Author

College Success Guaranteed: 5 Rules to Make It Happen

COLLEGE SUCCESS GUARANTEED 2.0

5 Rules for Parents

Malcolm Gauld

ROWMAN & LITTLEFIELD
Lanham • Boulder • New York • Toronto • Plymouth, UK

Published by Rowman & Littlefield
4501 Forbes Boulevard, Suite 200, Lanham, Maryland 20706
www.rowman.com

10 Thornbury Road, Plymouth PL6 7PP, United Kingdom

British Library Cataloguing in Publication Information Available

Library of Congress Cataloging-in-Publication Data

Library of Congress Cataloging-in-Publication Data Is Available
ISBN 978-1-4758-1073-8 (pbk. : alk. paper) — ISBN 978-1-4758-1079-0 (electronic)

∞™ The paper used in this publication meets the minimum requirements of American National Standard for Information Sciences Permanence of Paper for Printed Library Materials, ANSI/NISO Z39.48-1992.

Printed in the United States of America

To Gigi and Laurie,
My Sisters

CONTENTS

INTRODUCTION

Get yourself fired as a manager. . . . Then get rehired as a consultant.

- T. C. B.
- The 5 Rules for . . . Your Kids
- The Sequel: The 5 Rules for . . . *You*
- Things Have Changed
- Parents as Friends
- I'm Not the Only One
- A Suggested Frame of Mind for the Reader
- The Meter Starts Running at 30
- A Few Words about Bullshit
- Parent Stories and Anecdotes
- The Offer of the College

T. C. B.

Since I began teaching high school students nearly forty years ago, I have watched thousands of high school graduates head off to college. In my early years I didn't give it much thought. Although saddened to see the kids move on, I would refocus my attention on the new ones following behind. After a while, I couldn't help but notice some unmistakable patterns relating to my students after they hit college.

Another thing I noticed was my poor track record in predicting how my students would perform in college. I often found myself surprised . . . both ways. Some of the kids I was sure would excel would turn around and bomb. And some of the kids I was sure would bomb would surprise me by the extent to which they would buckle down and get after it. Before long I gave up predicting. Instead, I set my mind to trying to identify and understand the behaviors that the successful ones appeared to exhibit.

As a high school teacher of U.S. history and government, I would seek to personalize the three branches of U.S. government (i.e., executive, legislative, and judicial) by off-handedly asking my seniors, "So tell me, how's your executive function coming along?" I would then use their look of puzzlement as an unintended invitation to seize the liberty to tell them a bit more than they wanted to know:

"Yeah, well, you know, if your legislative function has to do with how well you're working with others, and your judicial function is all about whether you're acting wisely and honorably, your executive function is all about . . . T. C. B."

Correctly discerning that I was not about to back off, he or she would then usually take the bait: "Uhm . . . what do you mean by T. C. B., Mr. Gauld?"

I'd then reply, "I mean . . . Taking. Care of. Business."

I had come to realize T. C. B. is what success in college (and probably a very long list of other things) is all about. It's doing what you need to do when you need to do it. It's about the propensity to delay gratification when no adult authority figure is on the scene to remind (or *make*) you do whatever it is that you need to do. I can't vouch for how scientific this is, but I can say that kids who can master T. C. B. tend to do well in college and the kids who can't master T. C. B. tend to flounder. (And T. C. B. is also a very good post-college attribute to have!)

THE 5 RULES FOR . . . YOUR KIDS

About a decade ago, I began giving an annual talk to high school seniors in hopes of sending them off to college on a positive note. This led to my book *College Success Guaranteed: 5 Rules to Make It Happen* (2011).

My intention was to help college-bound students rise above the pitfalls waiting to snare them, the biggest one being the danger of drowning in free time. A close second lies in the failure to navigate the transition from *homework*, a short-term daily obligation (and a term they will never again hear after high school), to the long-term ongoing commitment of *studying*. And once again, this all circles back to the factor of how one handles free time.

As the title suggests, the book offers five rules to help the new college student begin and stay on track. In writing the book, I gathered anecdotes, tips, and strategies in interviews with college kids and recent grads from more than forty colleges and universities. Briefly, the five rules for college kids are:

*Rule No. 1 – Go to **Class***. Every kid I've ever known who flunked out of college failed to go to class. (And I've never known a kid to attend all of his or her classes and then fail.) High school penalizes you if you miss class; college may not even know if you're there. This is the most important rule, and yet, nonetheless, kids can have an amazing capacity to think that it doesn't apply to them.

*Rule No. 2 – **Study 3 Hours X 5 Days per Week***. You may need to do more to make Dean's List; you may even get away with less. (Note: One of my daughters seemed to take particular pleasure in scoffing, for my benefit, "Dad, I *never* do 15 hours per week." Meanwhile, the other would lament, "I could *never* get by with only 15." For what it's worth, they both did well.) My point is simply that if you study three hours per day (15 hours per week), regardless of whatever assignment might be due the following day, you'll do fine. Also, I've observed that the kids who will consistently do 15 hours are also the ones who will muster the initiative to jack it up to

20 or 25 when heavier work comes due. However, and here's the main point: Kids with *no* foundation of habit tend to flounder, freak-out, or both, once the academic pressure increases.

*Rule No. 3 – **Commit** to Something.* While it might seem counterin-tuitive, college students who stay busy tend to do better than those who don't. Whether on an athletic team, in a play, or on the college newspaper, not only will such activities *not* detract from your aca-demics, they will enhance them. It will also bring you into regular contact with other committed and industrious peers, causing you to establish a network that can prove to be of great mutual benefit in the decades after college.

*Rule No. 4 – Get a **Mentor**.* When I shared my book with University of Southern California Distinguished Professor of Business and leadership guru Warren Bennis, his first comment to me was, "I only disagree with one point you make in your book, Malcolm. You don't 'get' a mentor, you *stalk* mentors . . . and you stalk them your whole life!" High school teachers are expected to be on the lookout for kids who could use some extra help in their academic or person-al lives. In college, the burden falls on you, the student, to go out and make the connections that can propel you forward.

*Rule No. 5 – **Procrastination** Kills.* In one group interview I asked, "What is the one thing you would tell a college student beginning classes tomorrow?" One student in the group responded, "Procrasti-nation kills." All the other students in the room chuckled, and before long the room came alive with procrastination stories. Procrastina-tion: Deal with it before it deals with you!

Before launching into the five rules, both the book and my talks begin with three guidelines to set the stage:

First, *College Success Guaranteed: 5 Rules to Make It Happen* is a "do" book . . . not a "don't" book. I'm focused almost exclusively on the things you need to do. I figure that your parents, teachers, or relatives will fully cover all those things you shouldn't do. (I've also observed that if kids fully commit to the things they should do, they won't have nearly enough time to do those things they shouldn't.)

Second, after getting them to ponder the significance of the number 168, I offer a very precise estimate on what their weekly time commitment will be, right down to the number of hours: 27. Given the number of hours in a week—*168*—they'll still have 141 hours left over to use as they wish. They tend to like that idea.

Third, I ask them to consider a quote that I (believe I) originated: *Man is the only animal in the forest that bullshits himself.* Ours is the only species whose members regularly work against their own best interests through procrastination, over-eating, over-spending, under-exercising, and the like. And bullshit has an uncanny way of protecting itself. In fact, oftentimes, I have seen college students flunk out of college and wind up being the last to know that the ship has been going down for half the semester. So, *don't bullshit thyself.* The five rules are designed to prevent kids from doing just that. Rather than the be-all and end-all for everyone, they are offered as a tried-and-true system to help kids get off to a good start.

The Sequel: 5 Rules for . . . *You*

Since writing the original book, many parents have asked me for tips on how they might optimize their son or daughter's college experience. Hence, I began to devote a portion of my talks to offering five rules for *parents.*

After one of my talks, my father, an active educator with more than sixty years of experience working with students and families, observed that just about all of my "parent rules" had to do with "letting go." While I can't say that I originally intended that, I have to agree with him. If the most important priority for students is to go to class, then the most important priority for parents may well be to step aside and allow their kids to take the wheel.

On face value, this idea seems obvious and easy. However, in recent years I have observed countless parents struggle with it. Years ago, I heard parent/family expert Michael Riera focus this dynamic in a talk about the role of manager versus consultant relative to parenting (see www.mikeriera.com). Riera asked the parents of college-bound children to consider the idea that they had been their child's primary manager for eighteen years. He then called upon them to make sure that they got themselves fired (as manager) by the time they dropped said child off at college. (And if your child hasn't fired you, then resign.) While acknowledging this step as both sad and difficult, Riera said something to the effect of "If you play your cards right, you will eventually be re-hired as a *consultant*." He noted that being a consultant has it all over being a manager in so many ways, not the least of which is the fact that it frees you up to start thinking about how to get back to focusing on your own life!

As with the first book, the *College Success Guaranteed 2.0: 5 Rules for Parents* includes anecdotes and techniques gleaned from interviews I have conducted with parents who have sent children to college. At face value, they seem simple enough:

Rule No. 1 – Make Them Pay . . . for Something

Regardless of where you fall on the vast spectrum of financial means, your son or daughter ought to have some "skin in the game." I've observed that students who assume some financial responsibility for their education—anything from taking on partial loan obligations to expecting them to pay for books and clothes—generally perform better than those who don't. This chapter offers various models that parents have used in order to engage their children on the financial end of college.

Rule No. 2 – Wait for Their Call

Here's a simple test: After you drop off your child for new student orientation, have your next phone conversation be initiated by him or her. Resist the urge to call before you even get home. The mother of a Syracuse student, herself a social worker, told me about something she called the Pursuer-Distancer Dynamic: "When I pursued him with phone calls and e-mails, he resisted. Then when I stopped pursuing, he started calling me." She further observed, "I get a kick out of it when he calls and asks, 'Why haven't you called me?'" This chapter describes how some families have handled communication between home and the child who has left the nest for college.

Rule No. 3 – Step Aside

This rule calls upon you, the parent, to step aside and allow new mentors to enter your child's life. (Consider the possibility that your role may have even prevented your child from developing the ability to connect with mentors.) College offers a wealth of dynamic people who can make a huge difference in your child's life. Step aside and let it happen. This chapter shows how some parents have done that and describes mentor relationships that have evolved as a result.

Rule No. 4 – Mantra: Is This My Issue?

This rule is actually a mantra that I ask parents to internalize when they are engaged in communications with their college child. Should your child call with a complaint about his/her roommate or an overly demanding professor, ask yourself, "Is this my issue?" Try having your opening answer be "No." Several parents have shared stories describing how they have dealt with this.

Rule No. 5 – Get Curious

Any and all college websites tout the promise of graduating life-long learners. When you think about it, isn't that the point? While I don't believe he had children, author James Baldwin once said something I have used many times when working with families: "Children have never been very good at listening to their elders, but they never fail to imitate them." If you commit to being a life-long learner, you will be sending a powerful message to your child. Even if he/she jokes about it or scoffs at you, your kids are paying attention all the time, and that may be one of the greatest legacies you can give them. This chapter offers examples shared by parents.

THINGS HAVE CHANGED

The college application process has changed considerably over the course of my career, to say nothing of the days since I applied to college in 1972. While I was exploring/considering/applying to colleges as a high school senior, I really don't remember my parents involved at all. I went on all the campus visits either by myself or with friends and pretty much filled out all the applications with very little supervision. The college counselor at my high school was a wise and helpful man who invited us to come into his office anytime to explore the scores of view books and catalogs he had filed alphabetically (that is, at least until we got done with them!) on his book shelves. We would run ideas by him regarding schools and he would tell us what he knew and occasionally accompany his remarks with his frank assessment of our chances for admission. I emerged from the experience feeling pretty good with some appealing choices balanced with some disappointing rejections.

Today I don't see very many kids who do the college application experience the way my peers and I did. Perhaps the biggest change is simply the fact that parents are more involved than they have ever been. My study and teaching of history causes me to conclude that we are great pendulum swingers in this country.

As an example, many in my Baby Boomer generation felt that our fathers (especially) may not have been as involved in our lives as we might have wished. More than a few members of my peer group have lamented the fact that their fathers missed a lot of their sports games or other school events. Not only do today's fathers attend many more games than their fathers might have, they also make many of the *practices*. Some of this is good, but . . .

I believe that America's parenting pendulum has swung to an extreme degree of over-involvement. This is not to say that parents should stop going to their children's athletic games or that they should drop out of the application process entirely. However, I doubt that there has ever been a time when the demarcation line of who is responsible for what has ever been as blurred as it is now. This book is offered as a tool intended to help parents of college-bound children by presenting a possible framework to follow after their children have moved out of the house and on to the college campus of their choice.

PARENTS AS FRIENDS

Entering my third decade as a high school teacher in the late 1990s, I couldn't say why I cringed when I would hear teenagers refer to Mom or Dad as "my best friend." Everyone in the room would beam with warmth. To tell you the truth, it sounded like fingernails on a chalkboard to me.

On the one hand, it's a heart-warming sentiment. (I mean, what could be wrong with parents and children loving each other and spending a lot of quality time together?) On the other hand, assuming that our kids already have friends of their own . . . and assuming that the parents also have friends of their own . . . uhm . . . who's minding the store in the parenting department?

I've gone back and forth on this issue. Sometimes I have felt that my concerns about the over-engagement of parents are justified. And there have been a few times when I have felt as though I am a scrooge-like, cold-hearted curmudgeon placed on this earth to serve as a family buzz kill.

I'M NOT THE ONLY ONE

A few years ago, the cover of *Atlantic Monthly* magazine featured an illustration of a golden trophy inscribed with the citation "Good

Try." The feature article headline screams: "How the Cult of Self-Esteem is Ruining Our Kids." The main article, by Lori Gottlieb, is titled "How to Land Your Kid in Therapy—Why the Obsession With Our Kids' Happiness May Be Dooming Them to Unhappy Adulthoods."

Combining her research with that of several colleagues, Gottlieb makes some points that might strike some as counterintuitive. She:

argues that our obsession with happiness (and our warped understanding of it) is doing deep damage to our kids;

poses the idea that we may actually be spending *too much* time with our kids;

wonders if we are not serving our own emotional needs at the expense of our kids;

thinks we may be giving our kids too many choices.

Regarding happiness, Gottlieb writes, "The American Dream and the pursuit of happiness have morphed from a quest for general contentment to the idea that you must be happy at all times and in every way."[1]

She quotes Barry Schwartz, a professor at Swarthmore College: "Happiness as a byproduct of living your life is a great thing. But happiness as a goal is a recipe for disaster."[2] Gottlieb wonders, "Could it be that by protecting our kids from unhappiness as children, we're depriving them of happiness as adults?"[3]

Borrowing from UCLA psychologist Paul Bohn, Gottlieb utilizes the analogy of a young girl who trips and skins her knee. Making the case for moms and dads to resist the parental urge to immediately jump to the child's aid, Bohn observes,

> If you don't let her experience that momentary confusion, give her the space to figure out what just happened (Oh, I tripped), and then briefly let her grapple with the frustration of having fallen and perhaps even try to pick herself up, she has no idea what discomfort feels like, and will have no framework for how to recover when she feels discomfort later in life.[4]

Gottlieb argues that helping a child with a skinned knee seems like the right thing to do until "these toddlers become the college kids who text their parents with an SOS if the slightest thing goes wrong, instead of attempting to figure out how to deal with it themselves."[5]

In *Too Much of a Good Thing: Raising Children of Character in an Indulgent Age*, Harvard psychologist Dan Kindlon argues that the "psychological immunity" that kids must develop requires an acquaintance with painful feelings: "It's like the way our body's immune system develops. You have to be exposed to pathogens, or your body won't know how to respond to an attack. Kids also need exposure to discomfort, failure, and struggle." Otherwise, he maintains, "By the time they're teenagers, they have no experience with hardship."[6]

In the introduction to *Too Much of a Good Thing*, Kindlon writes:

> Compared to earlier generations, we are emotionally closer to our kids, they confide in us more, we have more fun with them, and we know more about the science of child development. But we are too indulgent. We give our kids too much and demand too little of them.

He then personalizes his observation:

> I find myself at the center of this problem as I try, with my wife, to balance the two major tasks of parenting: showing our kids that we love them and raising them with the skills and values they'll need to be emotionally healthy adults, which often requires that we act in ways that can anger and upset them.

Speaking to the solution to this dilemma, Kindlon writes: "When we stop blurring the line between friend and parent, we can help our kids develop healthy attitudes and good habits that are character's foundation."[7]

Lest anyone dismiss Kindlon as mired in the perspective of good old days that never were, he later writes:

I am not urging a return to the stereotypical family of the 1950s in which the father's word was law and physical punishment the remedy of choice for misbehavior. But the desire to form a close bond with our children should not come at the expense of not being able to set an unyielding limit or rule when a child needs it. [8]

Turning to the notion of quality time, Gottlieb observes,

> Back in graduate school, the clinical focus had always been on how the *lack* of parental attunement affects the child. It never occurred to any of us to ask, what if the parents are *too* attuned? What happens to *those* kids? [9]

These days, it has become a badge of parental honor to boast, "I never miss my kid's games." Just to offer the jolt of a different perspective, I like to urge parents to miss a game intentionally: "You'll definitely have something to talk about later." They invariably look at me as though I've been beamed down from Mars.

My point? Why are we *really* going to all the games? Does it fulfill a need that our child has? Or does it fulfill a need that *we* have?

Also quoted in the Gottlieb article, family psychologist Jeff Blume believes that "We're confusing our own needs with our kids' needs and calling it good parenting." He goes on to say,

> It's sad to watch. I can't tell you how often I have to say to parents that they're putting too much emphasis on their kids' feelings because of their own issues. If a *therapist* is telling you to pay *less* attention to your kid's feelings, you know something has gotten way out of whack. [10]

Turning to choice, Jean Twenge, coauthor of *The Narcissism Epidemic*, observes, "We treat our kids like adults when they're children, and we infantilize them when they're eighteen years old." [11]

Maybe we give our kids a lot of choices because we didn't have them growing up. However, Gottlieb notes, "We didn't expect so much choice, so it didn't bother us not to have it until we were older, when we were ready to handle the responsibility it requires."[12]

Gottlieb's motivation is fueled by too many patients who seem to love their parents but can't handle life. As a parent, which would you rather have: a teenager who occasionally professes dislike for you but grows into a well-adjusted thirty-year-old—or—a thirty-year-old who loves you but can't function as an adult?

If, like me, you're a Baby Boomer, you probably want both. So, stay focused on discipline and respect, and chances are you'll end up with a well-adjusted adult and a loving relationship. On the other hand, focus on nurturing a loving relationship and you may well end up with neither. And that's a lot worse than the sound of fingernails on a chalkboard.

Two more books that explore issues of over-parenting are A Nation of Wimps by Hara Marano and The Parents We Mean to Be by Richard Weissbourd. Both authors tip their hands with their subtitles: *The High Cost of Invasive Parenting* (Marano) and *How Well-Intentioned Adults Undermine Children's Moral and Emotional Development* (Weissbourd).

At one point, Marano refers to Harvard College's Handbook for Parents. Such handbooks have become common as colleges strive to find ways to facilitate critical separation between parent and student. (Marano notes the University of Vermont's use of "bouncers" to get parents off campus after student orientation has begun!) The challenge is magnified, Marano argues, due to the fact that the process of independence works best when it occurs gradually and occurs over many years from youth through adolescence. It's really not the kind of thing that one can do overnight, and the attempt to do it as a cram course can be traumatic for both child and parent. A rush job can be tantamount to today's minor cavity turning into tomorrow's root canal.

Weissbourd observes, "[I]n some cases young people can't separate [from their parents] because they have been infantilized by their parents from early ages and simply can't function on their own."[13] He examines what I call "The Cult of Self-Esteem" and what he calls the "Praise Craze." His research has caused him to take a dim view of the "parent as friend" approach that many of today's parents have attempted to use in raising their children.

There is another common parental utterance that also often hits me as fingernails-on-a-chalkboard. The setting usually finds me in conference with a student and his parents. Let's say we are discussing ways that Johnny might show improvement either academically or behaviorally. (Note: More often than not, the two are closely connected!) For me, the irksome moment occurs when one parent turns to Johnny and sincerely says, "Honey, I hope you know that my only hope is for you to be happy." Resisting the urge to wince, I then explore that parent's willingness to put that sentiment on hold for a bit in order for their child to do some "unhappy" things for a while in the hope that we can all work our way toward some happiness for *all* a little further on down the road. All the while, I know it's a tall order, especially if the parent's eyes lock with those of the child. After all, those eyes want unhappy things about as much as . . . well . . . a root canal.

Hey, we all want to be happy, but maybe George Orwell had it right: "Men can only be happy when they do not assume that the object of life is happiness."

Finally, in *How Children Succeed: Grit, Curiosity, and the Hidden Power of Character*, Paul Tough writes of what he calls "a central paradox of contemporary parenting":

> We have an acute, almost biological impulse to provide for our children, to give them everything they want and need, to protect them from dangers and discomforts both large and small. And yet we know—on some level, at least—that what kids need more than anything is a little hardship: some challenge, some deprivation that they can overcome, even if just to prove to themselves that they can.[14]

In researching his book, Tough spent a good deal of time at Riverdale Country School, a prestigious New York City day school. Tough quotes Riverdale head of school Dominic Randolph: "The idea of building grit and building self-control is that you get that through failure. And in most highly academic environments in the United States, no one fails anything."[15]

In any case, the above authors, all careful and committed students of human behavior, seem to agree that we have swung the pendulum to an over-engaged, over-protective extreme. I have included a bibliography of books on the topic.

A SUGGESTED FRAME OF MIND FOR THE READER

During my interviews, I began to notice a common theme expressed by parents who have sent multiple children to college. For example, one mother of three college children said, "You know, by the third child, *I learned*. I got smarter. I turned more of the responsibility for my kids' progress, success, and general happiness over to them. I realized that I too had a life and needed to get on with it. I may have learned it the hard way, but I definitely learned to step aside."

In reading this book, it is my hope that parents will avoid the temptation to compare themselves against the many examples and anecdotes that are offered here. Our current national culture seems to embody a counter-productive pull of a steady pressure to downplay our parenting foibles and missteps. We are supposed to know what to do in any and all circumstances. We are also supposed to make it appear as though we are doing it all effortlessly. It can even be seen as a weakness for us to ask for help.

Anyone who is good at anything—a premier athlete, a masterful courtroom attorney, a gifted teacher, a guitar god—has spent hours and hours learning from and consulting with others who excel at the same activity. Why would parenting be any different? Asking for help is a sign of strength. After all, anything that will move our kids forward is something any committed parent ought to want to know about. Who cares where or from whom it came?

So, I urge the reader to keep an open mind, and try to draw some wisdom from the experiences presented. Many of the anecdotes provided by parents were offered in the spirit of "If only I knew then what I know now." Like life itself, parenting must be lived forward but can only be understood in reverse.

I am especially grateful to the parents who gave me the unvarnished truth, who openly described the measures they took which were not effective as well as those that hit their mark as intended. I would submit that, if you are a parent of a child headed to college, you will likely do some of both. It is my hope that this book will help lead you to an approach that works for your child and for you.

THE METER STARTS RUNNING AT 30

Ironically, while I have spent my adult life working in a category of school referred to as "college preparatory," I do not see myself in the college preparation business. Sure, I want my students and your children to excel in college, but I certainly hope I'm in the *life* preparation business. I like to express to my colleagues, my students, and their parents my belief that "the meter starts running at 30." If the purpose of education is to prepare kids for life, well, there's a lot of life left after college. College can be a valuable and meaningful step along the way, but it is by no means the be-all and end-all.

The truth is, I've had many students who did very well in college who have yet to put their adult lives together in that mix of success and fulfillment we hope all our kids—be they our children or our students—will one day find. I've also had plenty who totally bombed college (some on more than one occasion) who today are knocking the proverbial cover off the ball in their personal, professional, and familial lives.

A FEW WORDS ABOUT BULLSHIT

In my book *College Success Guaranteed: 5 Rules to Make It Happen*, just prior to launching into my proposed five rules for college-bound students, I ask the reader to ponder a quote that I have shared for many years with Hyde School seniors on the eve of their graduation: "Man is the only animal in the forest that bullshits himself." Think about it.

As I write in *College Success Guaranteed*:

> Animals pretty much serve their best interests on a daily basis. They generally:
>
> > sleep when they're tired;
> > eat a healthy diet;
> > keep trim and stay in good physical condition;
> > have no problems with procrastination;
> > have a healthy and responsible sex life; etc.
>
> Men and women, on the other hand, often have trouble with the above to say nothing of other issues, especially when it comes to:
>
> > eating and drinking the right things;
> > getting enough sleep;
> > maintaining exercise routines;
> > sticking to schedules;
> > over-spending; etc.
>
> Animals in the wild *never* have those problems. (They also don't smoke . . . anything.) Not only do men and women have those problems on an all-too-frequent basis, we often delude ourselves into believing that we *don't* have them when we most certainly do.[16]

Of the kids I have known who have gone off to college and bombed, I have often observed that all too many of those young men and women have been the last to know when the ship is indeed going down. Sadly, right up until the eleventh hour, some will say to themselves, their friends, or their parents:

- "Plenty of kids miss a lot more classes than I do."
- "I don't party anywhere near as much as the hockey players do."
- "I'm really going to buckle down . . . *next* week."

- "Professor X never flunks anyone."
- "I already went over most of the class material in high school."

And so it goes until they find out too late that they have been bullshitting themselves the whole time, and they are the last to know.

The problem with bullshitting yourself is simply the fact that it's hard to know when you're doing it. (It's weird, but bullshit has an uncanny way of protecting itself.) And, dear parents, I would ask you to consider the idea that kids aren't the only ones capable of deluding themselves. As you read the five rules that form the core of this book, consider the idea that it can be easy for you to:

make yourself believe that your children are contributing to their educational *costs* when they're really not;
convince yourself that you're not badgering your child with phone *calls* and/or text messages (and as you will see, they can *really* be a problem!);
B.S. yourself into believing that you're *stepping aside* when nothing could be further from the truth;
assume far too much ownership of your *child's issues* while they're away at college;
play the martyr in addressing your child's "needs" or wants as a way to avoid *getting on with your own life.*

PARENT STORIES AND ANECDOTES

Much of the wisdom in the following pages comes from the parents of current and recently graduated college students from well over fifty different colleges and universities (see the full list in the section "Colleges and Universities") who were nice enough to share their successes and failures with me for your benefit. I simply sat down and talked with them, asked them some standard questions, and then listened and took a lot of notes.

The parents I spoke with covered a spectrum of socioeconomic circumstances, but it is fair to say that most came from backgrounds where the expectation of attending college was a given for them when they were young as well as for the children they have raised. Many are parents of children who have attended one of the Hyde Schools where I have taught, coached, and administrated for more than thirty-five years and where I currently serve as president (see www.hyde.edu).

The stories in this book have been presented anonymously. Any names that are mentioned have been changed. When appropriate, I have mentioned the name of the college or university where a given story took place, but have tried to use discretion in order to avoid any embarrassment on the part of any students, parents, or the schools themselves.

I do not guarantee that every piece of advice in this book will work for you. As a matter of fact, it's only fair for me to warn you that in offering up their stories, some of my interviewees served up ideas and suggestions that are contradictory. Thirty-five–plus years of working with kids and families have taught me that my chosen line of work is anything but an exact science. The success of my profession rests upon committed individuals and groups coming together to help each other in the hope that they, in turn, will pay it forward for the benefit of unknown and untold others. It is in this spirit that this book is offered.

THE OFFER OF THE COLLEGE

In September 1972, after I had hoisted my belongings up to my fourth floor Bowdoin College dormitory room, I found this formally printed statement waiting on my desk:

The Offer of the College

To be at home in all lands and all ages;
To count Nature a familiar acquaintance,
And Art an intimate friend;

To gain a standard for the appreciation of others' work
And the criticism of your own;
To carry the keys of the world's library in your pocket,
And feel its resources behind you in whatever task you undertake;
To make hosts of friends . . .
Who are to be leaders in all walks of life;
To lose yourself in generous enthusiasms
And cooperate with others for common ends—
This is the offer of the college for the best four years of your life.

This brilliant piece was written by William DeWitt Hyde, president of Bowdoin College from 1885 through 1917. I'd like to tell you that I read Hyde's piece, pondered it deeply, and discussed it at length that freshman year with my peers, all of whom also received it on their desks. But, I did not. Yet more than forty years later it has a deep meaning to me, especially given that one of my daughters has recently graduated from the same institution and received the benefit of the same offer. May this offer visit your children during their college years and beyond.

In order for your child to gain the full value of the offer of his or her college, I urge you to step aside and allow it to happen. Hopefully, as a parent, you have already stepped aside while your children have experienced both success and failure. If this is true, then I congratulate you for advancing against the wind of the prevailing culture. If not, well, I hope the following pages will assist you in taking this critical step in your parenting.

And one more thing for those who count themselves among the stepped aside group: Well . . . there's no nice way to say this. . . . It could also be that you're bullshitting yourself. I've observed that kids have nothing on parents when it comes to maintaining high levels of self-deception. I've known many, many parents who have espoused the belief that they had "let go" of their children despite the fact that no innocent bystander would think so.

Regardless of where you fall, it is my hope that the 5 Rules for Parents, when added to the 5 Rules for Students, will offer a one-two punch for your family for "the best four years of your life" and for many years to come.

NOTES

1. Lisa Gottlieb, "How to Land Your Kid in Therapy—Why the Obsession With Our Kids' Happiness May Be Dooming Them to Unhappy Adulthoods," *Atlantic Monthly* magazine (June 7, 2011).
2. Ibid.
3. Ibid.
4. Ibid.
5. Ibid.
6. Dan Kindlon, *Too Much of a Good Thing: Raising Children of Character in an Indulgent Age* (New York: Hyperion, 2001), introduction.
7. Ibid.
8. Ibid., 21.
9. Gottlieb.
10. Ibid.
11. Jean Twenge, *The Narcissism Epidemic: Living in the Age of Entitlement* (New York: Free Press, 2009).
12. Ibid.
13. Richard Weissbourd, *The Parents We Mean To Be: How Well-Intentioned Adults Undermine Children's Moral and Emotional Development* (New York: Mariner Books, 2010), 89.
14. Paul Tough, *How Children Succeed: Grit, Curiosity, and the Hidden Power of Character* (New York: Mariner Books, 2012), 109–10.
15. Ibid.
16. M. Gauld, *College Success Guaranteed: 5 Rules to Make It Happen* (Lanham, MD: Rowman & Littlefield Education, 2011), introduction.

Rule No. 1

MAKE THEM PAY . . . FOR SOMETHING

People who pay full price never complain. It's the feller you try
to give something to that you can't ever please. —Will Rogers,
American humorist (1879–1935)

My Take:

- Times Ten+

Parent Stories & Anecdotes:

- Wonderful Sounding Board
- Comparing Costs *before* Choosing Where to Enroll
- No Credit Cards
- Payment for Credits Earned
- Our Gift: A Loan-Free Education
- Doubling Summer Earnings
- Undergraduate versus Graduate Support
- Parents of Substantial Means
- Student Loans
- Used Books
- Payment for Four Years . . . and Four Years Only
- A Son Does It on His Own
- Funding Four College Kids

- When the First Attempt Fails

MY TAKE

Times Ten+

The opening lines in my book *College Success Guaranteed: 5 Rules to Make it Happen* may be a good way to begin this chapter:

> So, you're headed off to college. . . . Congratulations! Looks like those twelve-plus years of school are about to pay off . . . Big Time! You should feel proud.
>
> So, tell me, are you ready? I mean, really ready?
>
> Before you answer, I feel compelled to warn you that a lot of things have changed since I was in college in the mid-1970s. (And in case you're wondering, *No*, I was not ready.) Without offering up a list here, I'll just point out what is maybe the most glaring difference: The cost . . . has increased . . . more than tenfold.
>
> To dramatically illustrate, my daughter and I share the same alma mater. What my parents spent (combined with my college loans) to send me there for one year will not cover my daughter's costs . . . for one month. [1]

After I wrote those lines, I realized that if you added a zero to my mid-1970s tuition bill, you'd still be $10,000 short of the bill our family received for my daughter's final year in college.

When I stand before an audience of new college parents, I can be assured of the fact that these parents represent a wide spectrum of financial means. For some, maybe the majority, the cost of the college will be a highly taxing, if not monumental, challenge. However, there will also likely be some parents present for whom it's simply a matter of pulling out the checkbook and writing a check without a moment's thought. Regardless of where you fall on the spectrum of financial means, it is important for your son or daughter to have some "skin in the game." Everybody I have spoken with and all the studies I've observed strongly suggest that students who have some financial responsibility for their education will likely perform better than those who don't.

One sentiment I heard expressed regularly in my interviews was along the lines of how "College is so expensive these days that there's absolutely no way a kid could work his or her way through college as some in my generation did." Some of the strongest proponents of this viewpoint were, in fact, parents who had indeed worked their own way through college. While there's no question that it's expensive, my discussions revealed some exceptions to the current conventional wisdom.

In fact, I was surprised to encounter some circumstances of individuals who navigated their way to a college degree completely on their own and without crushing student loans after it was all over. They tended to enroll in state universities and they just made it happen in their own ways on whatever schedules suited their circumstances, in defiance of common paradigms of how one is "supposed" to do college.

For example, they might have held down jobs as much as they studied, thereby stretching the experience over five or more years. To the casual observer, they may have looked more like working people who happened to be taking a few classes as opposed to college students working part-time, but they obviously didn't care. For them, the four-year "norm" meant nothing. As one observed, "Hey, it's not like there are any jobs waiting out there for college grads anyway."

I also learned of students who combined military service with their college educations, earning credits and/or scholarships in the process. Some of these folks went this route after a failed first attempt at college, mixing a bit of the "School of Hard Knocks" into their education. I must say, a number of these folks exhibit impressive profiles today, some even more so than some of their peers who did college in the traditional four-year straight shot. (And think about this: Which candidate might look more impressive at a job interview?)

These examples are not intended to minimize the magnitude of today's costs. In fact, over the years some of my advice to high school seniors has changed in light of this cost. In the past when the idea of taking a year off before starting college would come up, I tended to advise against it. I felt that kids should just take the plunge and get on with it. (Perhaps I was influenced by my own experience that featured two very mediocre years at the start followed by a much stronger finish.) Today I tend to regularly tell kids and families on the fence to consider doing something else for a while. There are far less expensive places to go if you need to "find yourself."

As a child of the 1960s, I still chuckle whenever I see the film *Animal House* and hear John Belushi sigh, "Seven years of college down the drain." Today, I think seven years can actually be a good strategy, provided it's intentional from the start.

It only took a few interviews with parents to learn that there are as many ways to pay for college—and as many ways to get your child to participate in that responsibility—as there are college families. To be sure, I observed some common themes, but each and every family seems to put a unique spin on some aspect of the ordeal. Here are some of the approaches I encountered.

PARENT STORIES AND ANECDOTES

Wonderful Sounding Board

The mother of a first-year Clark University student said,

> My daughter received a merit scholarship and some need-based financial aid. She also took out loans and has a work-study job. I am paying very little, and Ava understands the debt is hers to carry when she graduates. I can't say enough about the value of the work-study job. Ava is working in the International Student Affairs office as a receptionist and is meeting wonderful mentors. The ladies in the office love to comment on her clothes, etc., and are a wonderful sounding board for her. I am embracing

the "Step Aside" advice. This is fabulous as I am well aware that I do not know everything, and I have come to accept that I do not always give the best advice. It allows Ava the experience of adults with strengths that differ from my own. What a gift!

Comparing Costs *before* Choosing Where to Enroll

The father of a daughter who had just begun her studies at Sacred Heart University in Connecticut told me how the issue of cost entered into his and his family's decision-making process before his daughter had even graduated from high school. He said,

> Both my wife and I paid our own ways through college. Given the astronomical rise in tuitions and other costs of a college education today, we knew that wasn't realistic for our daughter. So, we figured that we would pay half and our daughter would pay the other half. However, the closer we got to the starting line, the more we came to realize that even this scheme wasn't very realistic either.
>
> So, we basically resigned ourselves to pretty much paying for everything with the exception of a Stafford Loan that would leave our daughter with a long-term loan of approximately $30,000 after she graduated. Spaced out over several years, this seemed fair and right to all concerned.
>
> Then, in the middle of our discussions, our daughter told us that she was still thinking about attending a different school. While she described this school as her dream school, it soon became clear that she had not thought through the ramifications of the fact that it was also considerably more expensive. When I brought this to her attention, she got angry with me. After reminding her that there is nothing in any parental contract that requires me to pay for *any* college at all, I informed her that she was welcome to attend this other school provided she was also prepared to assume responsibility for the shortfall of approximately $100 thousand (over her four years) which would triple, if not quadruple her post-college loan obligation. She thought about it for a few days and then told me how excited she was to be attending Sacred Heart in the fall.

No Credit Cards

A mother of three college students told me that she and her husband made a simple decision that they would not give any of their children a credit card when they went to college. While the family certainly had the means to provide and cover a credit card for their children, they decided not to do so. Many times their children would come home from college and complain that they were the only ones in their dormitory who did not have a credit card. Several years later they pointed to that fact as a positive influence on their academic performance and claimed that it helped them develop a healthier relationship with money in general after they graduated. Shortly after graduating, one of them said, "Boy, a lot of my friends are going out into the world with pretty screwed up finances due to way too much credit card debt. Thanks for not allowing me to fall into that trap."

Payment for Credits Earned

I spoke with the mother of a University of Montana graduate who described a simple rule that she and her husband had relative to financing their child's education: "However many credits you earned last semester is how many we will pay for next semester. Fail to get a credit—you won't get compensated for that one the next semester and you'll have to make that credit up somewhere, somehow at your own expense."

On the one hand, as the parent, you might well choose to have a higher top line than that one. On the other hand, that policy features a pretty solid bottom line!

In a similar vein, the mother of three college students told me,

> We didn't put a lot of demands on our college children. In fact we might have been a bit soft, but we did make it clear that they needed to maintain a decent GPA. We never really stipulated what the exact number would be, but I think they got the message that it needed to be in the B or 3.0 range, and if it wasn't,

there needed to be a very good reason. For example, maybe they were engaged in a particularly challenging course. While we paid for everything, if it was clear that they had no interest in studying, we made it clear to them that we would yank the tuition payments, and I believe they got the point.

Another mother of three college students told me about a simple rule that might be described as a Flunk Fee. While each child was expected to cover his or her own books and spending money, Mom and Dad covered the tuition with one proviso: You must pay for any course you flunk. They described a circumstance when one of their daughters dropped a course late during a semester. While the student did not get an actual F on her transcript, the course was paid for. Hence, these parents required their daughter to make up the course at a local public university, at her expense, during the summer.

Our Gift: A Loan-Free Education

In our home, my wife and I tried to ensure that our two daughters would graduate from college without future loan obligations. In some ways, this may not have been all that rational given that both my wife and I left college with loan obligations and today believe we were the better for it. Some of our reasoning may have had something to do with the fact that their younger brother is on the autism spectrum and received a great deal of our time and resources growing up. (His sisters jokingly—and lovingly!—like to refer to him as "The Chosen One.") In any case, our daughters were on the hook for their books, their clothes, and their spending money, and they knew that this was not open for discussion. While we fronted them a few loans from time to time, we have insisted that these be paid back, and this has worked well.

Finally, one factor that has made this arrangement easier on their mother and me is the simple fact that both daughters have done well in college. I always feel for parents who are making major sacrifices in order for their children to attend college while their children fail to reciprocate with commensurate sacrifices of their own. I strongly urge such parents to consider the idea of terminating the arrangement—whatever it may be—and also consider the idea of requiring their children to work for a while and maybe restart college again sometime down the road. It might well serve their deepest interests to get out in the world and see with their own eyes exactly what is waiting for them.

The mother of a Providence College student told me of the approach her family used. She and her husband had originally intended to have their daughter assume some financial loans in order to own some of her education. However, in the midst of their planning, the daughter's grandfather announced his plans to set aside a trust fund for each of his grandchildren. Obviously, all were delighted to hear this news. However, the grandfather's plans also included an unexpected and interesting caveat: "My gift to your children, my grandchildren, is contingent upon the understanding that they will graduate from college loan-free." The message was clear to the parents: *You get them through college. . . . I will enhance their financial stability after they finish. But I don't want my grand-children getting out of college owing a lot of money.*

The grandfather had no problems with his grandchildren owning part of their education and being responsible for their finances, but he was adamant about them having no loans. In this case, he was fully in favor of his granddaughter struggling to make ends meet during college, but wanted her to have a fresh start after it was over.

Therefore, this mother and her husband found other ways to bring their daughter into the financial obligations of college. She would be held responsible for her own clothes and spending money. She would be on her own as far as owning a car (during or after college), and she was encouraged to have a work-study job at school. The mother said, "It has worked well. Put it this way, our daughter is about to graduate from Providence with a great GPA and is excited to head out into the world."

Doubling Summer Earnings

The mother of three college students told me about a simple formula related to helping her children with spending money while they were in college. Each child was expected to get a summer job to earn spending money. However, rather than dictate how much they would be expected to earn, she and her husband simply offered to double however much they had earned (and saved) by August 15. Then the total dollar amount equaled the cash they would have access to during the course of the entire school year.

The mother explained,

> We offered each kid two choices: (1) lump sum or (2) monthly disbursements. Our oldest chose lump sum and burned through it all by Christmas of his freshman year. He had to work all Christmas break just to get enough spending money to get him through the year. After that, he and all the kids who followed him to college chose the monthly disbursement option!

Mom concluded, "Our system has worked well for our family because it incentivizes them in two ways: (1) It makes them want to work, and (2) It makes them want to save."

Undergraduate versus Graduate Support

The mother of four college graduates explained the straightforward system of financial support she and her husband have utilized: "We offered to pay 100 percent of their college tuition and room and board. We offered to pay 50 percent of the graduate school bill. That has worked well for our family."

Parents of Substantial Means

I spoke with a mother of three college students who made an interesting observation:

If you are a parent of substantial means, the "Make Them Pay" rule can be a very hard one to follow. You can't, with a straight face, say to your kids, "This experience is really tapping us out. We need you to appreciate the deep sacrifice we are making." They know it's not true. And if you live in a neighborhood with families of similar means, the kids can reinforce each other in the misbelief that life is one big Easy Street.

I suspect that the majority of parents in America, like me, might not relate all that much to this predicament. For us, college costs put a pinch on our lifestyles. But once again, regardless of where you fall, it is important that your children own part of their education.

The same mother told me that she and her husband paid for everything when it came to the tuition, rooming expenses, food, and basic incidentals. What she did do, she said, is

> try to make them a little hungry. I did give my children a spending allowance, but it was always a little less than what they wanted, because I wanted them to feel forced to make choices. In other words, I can go to this concert next Saturday night or I can buy this cool-looking blouse, but I can't do both.

Interestingly enough, two of her children found jobs while in college, one as a baby-sitter, the other as a restaurant hostess. While it is true that they were receiving an allowance that was higher than the one most of their peers were receiving from their parents, it began to occur to them that they desired even more disposable income. The mother told them, "Your current allowance level is not going to increase, but you are certainly free to go out and earn more disposable income." And two of them chose to do exactly that.

The mother explained, "Their father and I certainly had the means to have given them a higher allowance at no sacrifice to ourselves, but we found that if they were given a little less than they wanted, they were often motivated to become more industrious in support of their own interests."

The mother of two college students told me:

We made it clear to both our boys that we would cover tuition, room, and board. We helped them with their spending money but it quickly dawned on them that they would not be able to live lavishly on what we gave them. When our oldest son made some good money during two consecutive summers of a well-paying job, he (and we) learned that he cared a lot more about the money he earned, and spent it more wisely, than the money we gave him.

She continued,

Now our older son is in law school, and we're helping him as we did when he was in college. His father and I laugh at some of his expensive tastes, such as sending his dry cleaning out. We told him that we think he ought to just go with wash-and-wear and hold off on the dry cleaning until he's pulling down the big bucks in a law firm. However, we're fine with him sending his clothes out . . . so long as he understands that we aren't paying for it. Simply put, our offer of financial support is good for tuition, but not dry cleaning.

The parents of three college graduates told me, "We probably should have set something up that would have challenged our kids to have some skin in the game, but we didn't." The father said, "I didn't even get to go to college, and my wife graduated with fairly substantial loan obligations, so we didn't want our kids to have to deal with all that. Our approach worked out great for the first two kids, but the third one had difficulties buckling down. We may well have made things a bit too easy for him."

Student Loans

A mother and father of three private college graduates told me that their cash flow made it impossible for them to pay their children's tuitions on time, especially given that during the nine-year span their children were in college, there were several years when at least two of them were enrolled at the same time. Therefore, they had their children take out some loans to help cover the costs. (They estimate that these loans may have amounted to 10 percent of the total cost of the tuitions they paid.) Then when their children graduated, the parents' graduation gift was the promise to pay off those loans for them. Talking with these parents it seemed this arrangement gave them peace of mind in that they were able to finance the education but also fulfill their original promise of providing a college education for their children.

Another mother and father of three college students told me that each of their children were expected to take out loans of $5,000 for each of the four years they were in college, putting each of them on the hook for $20,000 upon graduation. The mother said, "I'm not sure that any of our kids really got this obligation while they were actually enrolled in college. However, our oldest recently said, 'Oh, no! My first loan payment is due next month!' Suffice it to say that she's feeling it now!"

This mother went on to say, "We feel that this loan amount is a healthy reminder of the cost of their opportunity and their burden is by no means a crushing one, just enough to bring a healthy sense of urgency to their efforts to seek employment."

Used Books

The parents of three college graduates, all from private institutions, told me that they covered books and computers in the first semester. "Then," as the mother observed, "we learned about used books." This option offers the opportunity to purchase or perhaps even rent the required textbooks at a fraction of the cost of new ones. The family noted that at no time did they provide any spending money for any of their children; they were on the hook for this.

Payment for Four Years . . . and Four Years Only

The parent of a recent graduate from the University of Vermont told me that he and his wife pretty much covered all expenses for the first two years and then expected their children to shoulder the responsibility for incidentals and extra spending money beginning in their junior year. He also told me that he sat his son down at the beginning of his college experience and told him that he was willing to pay for four consecutive years of college and four consecutive years only. Then he told me that at one point his son dropped a course and in order for his father to pay for it, he had to take an extra course in a future semester to make up for it. I thought it was interesting because this policy discouraged the son from spreading college out over a long period of time. Hence, it did mandate some fiscal responsibility on his son's part.

Similarly, I spoke with the parents of three college graduates who covered all of their children's costs, including most of the incidentals, but they had one clear caveat: "Our offer is good for four years, and four years only." One of their children fell behind on credits and near the end of his college days he faced a dilemma: *Do I carry my credit issues over to a ninth semester?*—or—*Do I suck it up and shift into overdrive in order to get it all done in the spring of my senior year?* Given the conditions of his parents' support, he chose the latter and graduated on time with his friends.

A Son Does It on His Own

The mother of a University of Maine graduate told me:

> Just as my son was headed to college, his father died. And for a variety of reasons, a new marriage among them, I was unable to offer much financial support for his college education. I basically said to him, "You're on your own."
>
> Although we are Maine residents, the University of New Hampshire was actually closer to our home than our own state university. After being accepted at both, my son chose UNH; adding further to his challenges was the burden of an out-of-state tuition three times the cost of staying in-state. But he was determined.

Then just as the fall semester was to begin, my son came to the realization that his heart had ruled his head in making his decision. He wasn't sure that UNH was three times more valuable than UMaine and after calculating his post-graduation loan obligation, he chose to defer his admission to UNH in hopes of re-instating his admission to UMaine.

The following semester he indeed enrolled at UMaine, spending four very productive years there. He did it all on his own. In fact, I never saw a grade report from UMaine. It was truly his education.

This mother went on to tell a fascinating story about her son's initiative and character near the end of his college years. Having been an accomplished athlete in high school, he had grown to regret his decision to forsake varsity sports in order to hold down enough jobs to earn his way through school. However, during his off-hours, he had played in enough pick-up games with members of the UMaine varsity basketball team to believe that he could play at that caliber. Encouraged by team members to give it a shot, he told his mother about his plans to maybe "walk on" at a try-out. His mother responded, "I think you should go for it. In fact, I will pay for the semester so you don't need to work." Both mother and son were excited about this idea.

A week or so later, her son called home and announced, "I've changed my mind. I can't hang that unexpected obligation on you. It just doesn't feel right. I've done this by myself until now. I think I'll finish it off that way." He never brought up the idea again.

This mother had mixed feelings regarding her son's decision. On the one hand, knowing how important sports had been to her son, she was sorry he was not going to be taking his shot. On the other hand, she was proud of her son's decision-making process. As she noted, "We were always open with our kids about our financial circumstances. He knew where we were financially, and I think he just didn't want to add to the expense side of our financial budget."

Funding Four College Kids

One of my most interesting interviews was with the mother and father of four college students. Their first child entered college in 2005, their last in 2014. During most years they had two children enrolled at the same time. When child number one chose a private New England liberal arts college, both parents were understandably excited.

Mom observed,

> With the first kid we were cutting our teeth, so to speak. We paid for everything because we thought that's what we were supposed to do. Ironically, she was probably the least appreciative of our four kids. (In fact, her siblings like to rib her by calling her Princess Rebecca.) It's not so much a reflection of her character as the fact that we simply did too many things for her in terms of financial obligations.

This mother's comment brings to mind a quote attributed to American humorist Will Rogers (1879–1935): "People who pay full price never complain. It's the feller you try to give something to that you can't ever please."

With each successive child enrolling in college, this couple has increasingly transferred more and more financial responsibility to their children. Consequently, each child has become more economically self-sufficient.

When the First Attempt Fails

The mother of two college graduates told me that when she and her husband sent their first child off to college, they paid for everything. Not only did they feel a sense of parental obligation, they took pride in their ability to offer such a wonderful opportunity to their children. No sooner did their son arrive at Syracuse University before he got in over his head with an unbalanced separation between studying and socializing. After the first semester he found himself on academic probation. At the end of the second, the university mandated that he take a year off, reassess his priorities, and apply for readmission.

At this point, his parents felt that they had made a mistake by making his college opportunity a bit too easy for him. Hence, they chose to cut him off financially. Strongly desiring the opportunity to earn his way back to Syracuse, the son told his parents that he wanted to remain in the Syracuse area, get a job, and take courses at a community college. He reasoned that this would enable him to earn the credits he had missed, while hopefully also giving him the chance to return to Syracuse as a student in good standing.

His parents responded, "Well, since we're cutting you off, you have every right to proceed as you wish." While privately doubting that their son would follow through on his intentions, they decided to sit back and wait. Lo and behold, their son turned around and did exactly as he stated he would do: He enrolled in community college, buckled down, did some solid academic work, and earned his return back into Syracuse.

This experience with their son caused these parents to take a different approach with their daughter. When she headed off to college, they adopted a stance where they would continue to pay tuition but would hold their children responsible for clothes and spending money. This arrangement seemed to work better for both students. The mother said, "Our initial experience with our older child, although difficult for the whole family, taught us some important lessons about personal ownership and was better for all concerned."

Another mother told me of her experiences when her daughter wanted a second chance at college. On the first go-around she failed to get her priorities straight and was forced to return home. Her parents made it clear that she would need to get a job and experience the working world.

After a semester of working, she informed her parents that she felt she was ready to give it another shot. The parents, uncomfortable with the idea of their daughter returning to the same school and peer group, asked her to transfer to a different school. Even after their daughter successfully gained admission to a university closer to home, they were still hesitant. Therefore, they issued a clear ultimatum to their daughter: "We will fund the first semester. If you complete that first semester with a B average, we will continue to pay for your education."

Their daughter enrolled and completed the semester with an A and two Bs. As the mother said, "Our daughter was proud of her performance. We were also proud of her and happy for her. And beyond that, we felt very good about our investment and confident about moving forward."

NOTE

1. M. Gauld, *College Success Guaranteed: 5 Rules to Make It Happen* (Lanham, MD: Rowman & Littlefield Education, 2011), introduction.

Rule No. 2

WAIT FOR THEIR CALL

I know that things are going well when I don't hear from my daughter. —Mother of two college students

The phone is not really a problem. . . . The problem is all about the *texting*. —Mother of two college students

In the end, after three kids in college, I've learned two things. First, *I* have a life, and I need to begin to live it. Second, they can handle just about everything that comes up. —Mother of three college graduates

My Take:

- If You Don't Wait... You Might Embarrass Your Child

Parent Stories & Anecdotes:

- Sometimes "It Hurts"
- The Value of Distance
- Pursuer-Distancer Dynamic
- Boys versus Girls
- It's All about the Texting
- One More Rule: CELEBRATE!!!

- Cringe-Worthy
- Cell Phones
- Don't Fix . . . Ask Questions
- The Critical First Two Weeks
- Choosing "Hands Off"
- Wait to Hear from Them
- Try *Not* Taking Their Call
- Lessons from Sleep-Away Camp
- Catch-as-Catch-Can
- Where's the Bread?
- Let Me Tell You What's Going On with Me
- "Whatever You Do . . . Turn Around"

MY TAKE

When I recently spoke with the parents of new students at Southern New Hampshire University during the wrap-up to new student orientation, I offered a simple recommendation: "Knowing that you will probably want to talk on the phone before you even get out of the parking lot outside this building, I offer you a challenge: How about waiting for them to call you?"

When I went to college, I don't know that I spoke to my own parents before a couple of weeks went by, and it was basically a weekly phone call thereafter, but parents are much more involved today than they were a generation ago. And what's more, cell and smart phones provide so many more options in communicating: phone calls, texting, social media, and the like.

In her book *Nation of Wimps*, Hana Marano writes, "Think of the cell phone as the eternal umbilicus. It is the new pervasive instrument of overprotection."[1]

Before the cell phone, students had to work a lot of things out on their own. Say you got a bad grade on a test. First, you had to sit with it a while. You might go through a phase where you kept it to yourself. Then you might have sidled up to a peer and asked, "I bombed on this thing. How did you do?" Then you might have mustered up enough nerve to see your professor during his or her office hours. This progression was an important rite of passage for all college students. They had to work it out. Today, not only do many students in this same predicament bypass all of the above in favor of a call home to Mom, they may well be on that call before they have even gotten outside of the classroom building.

Marano observes that at the turn of the century about 38 percent of college kids had cell phones.[2] Today, do you know a college kid without one? College is supposed to be a dramatic plunge into a new and unfamiliar world. The lessons learned as a result of fighting to the surface are life-long. It's hard to plunge into a new world if you stay tethered to your old and familiar one. And that can be a problem with cell phones, computers, Facebook, and the like.

Marano laments that the cell phone impedes personal and psychological development because it "provides an excuse for first-year students not to have to get out and make new friends and new connections on campus." As a result, "socialization is restricted to comfortable old networks. You never have to learn how to get along with others or—God forbid—learn *from* others."[3]

So, wait for their call. Sure, you'll want to talk. And you will. But hold back a bit, especially in the early going, and give them the chance to be pioneers as they blaze a new trail and settle into a new home in a new, unfamiliar world.

If You Don't Wait . . . You Might Embarrass Your Child

While conducting interviews for this book, a friend told me a story of a young acquaintance's first day at an Ivy League university. The young man had spent his first day involved in freshman orientation activities. He'd had a few meals, met some professors, made some new friends, and after socializing at an informal mixer, he made his way back to his dormitory at 1:00 AM, not a wholly unusual hour for a young college student with no classes the next day.

Feeling good about his first day and confident that he had made a solid first impression on peers and faculty members, he was all set to climb into bed for the night. No sooner had he shut off the light and crawled into bed when he heard a knock on his door. He opened it to find his next door neighbor and a large contingent of dormitory mates standing there. His neighbor then proceeded to inform him of the fact that Campus Security had recently stopped by the dorm inquiring as to his whereabouts.

Apparently, this young man's mother had tried to call him and was highly concerned by his failure to pick up the phone at such a late hour. Hence, she had called the campus police to check on his safety.

While my friend and I chuckled about the story, I immediately thought about that recurring section of *Sports Illustrated* called "Signs of the Apocalypse." It is unfathomable to me that a parent would act in such a way after a child had gone to college. It's hard to believe that only two generations ago young men of the same age risked their lives while storming the beaches of Normandy. I can't help but feel that this parent's actions are an insult to those men. (Try this experiment: Watch the first 30 minutes of the film *Saving Private Ryan*. Then think about this story.)

PARENT STORIES & ANECDOTES

Sometimes "It Hurts"

One mother I interviewed, told me of her experiences communicating with her two children while they were in college. At one point she said, "I know that things are going well when I don't hear from my daughter. I don't text or call her during the academic week. When she first got to college, I used to let her vent her frustrations to me over the phone. I would then make suggestions, many of which back-fired. I concluded that I needed to back off. That has worked much better for both of us."

Changing topics to her communications with her son, she mentioned how she had told him about her own college days and how she generally called home every Sunday night:

> So, I asked him, "How about we talk on Sunday nights?" He responded with, "No, that's too often." Then, thinking I'm being especially magnanimous, I said, "OK, How about just every once in a while?" He then said, "Maybe. We'll see . . . " Sometimes he does call me, but it's not as often as I would like. And it hurts. But it seems to work. And when we do talk, the conversations are meaningful for both of us. At the end of the day, he's getting a great education, and that's the whole idea. My feelings about it have to take a back seat for now.

The Value of Distance

The mother of a Clark University student wrote,

> Wait for her to call. . . . Hmm . . . very difficult, especially those first weeks. My daughter and I are very close. As much as I miss her, I know that the relationships she has with adults at her school are better thanks to my distance from her. And how will she ever learn to ask for the things she needs if I am forever asking her if she needs anything? The trouble is that I miss her, which might mean that I need to "get curious"!

More on this when we get to Rule No. 5.

Pursuer-Distancer Dynamic

The mother of a Syracuse University student told me about the concept she calls the Pursuer-Distancer Dynamic. She found that when she pursued her child with phone calls and e-mails he resisted. Then when she stopped pursuing, he started calling. She also said, "I get a kick out of it when he calls me and asks, 'Why haven't you called me?'"

Another mother, one who has sent four children to college, seemed to be channeling this Syracuse mother when she told me, "We wait for them to call us. Sometimes the wait has been long, but we found that when we got into a pattern of calling them all the time, they almost never called us back."

Regarding the Pursuer-Distancer Dynamic, the mother of two college graduates told me,

> I learned early on that the more I called them, the less they called me. While I didn't plan this, over the six years that my two children were in college, the balance shifted over time from me calling them to them calling me. I found that giving them space early on led to frequent and deep talks later.

My experience working with families suggests that it's in the DNA of parents to want to give advice to their children. And it may even well be in the DNA of teenagers to resist it. In any case, while it might not have been mentioned by name, the Pursuer-Distancer Dynamic came up many times in my discussions with parents.

Boys versus Girls

The mother of two college boys said, "While my friends with daughters have told me unbelievable stories about talking and/or texting with their girls several times daily, whenever either my husband or I get a call from our sons, the other will exclaim, 'Really?!? Wait, you *actually* talked to him? What did he have to say?'"

The mother went on to say,

> In the early days we had anxiety over how seldom we would talk, but we decided to leave it up to them and get on with our own lives. As a result, months can go by without speaking. It doesn't feel good sitting around waiting, and so we stopped worrying about it. It's developmentally appropriate for them to be spreading their own wings. It may be a bit painful, but it's necessary. We know we have a deep bond with both our sons and we trust that will come back around.

It's All about the Texting

The mother of a Providence College student told me, "The phone is not really a problem. . . . The problem is all about the *texting*." Sensing my puzzlement, she went on to say,

> Thanks to texting, my daughter and I got into an unhealthy pattern where she would text me as soon as she rolled out of bed in the morning, and we would trade texts through much of the day. Then we would talk nearly every day at 5:00 in the afternoon, and neither of us would have anything to say.

The mother further explained,

> I was a nervous wreck. My daughter might text me in the morning and say, "I don't feel good today." That would set me off, and I would be churning all day as I texted her with questions such as:
>
> Did you take your Motrin today?
> Did you get enough sleep?
> Are you drinking enough liquids?
> Shouldn't you go to the campus health center?
>
> And this would go on all day—back and forth, back and forth.
> Then when I would call her at 5:00, I would anxiously ask, "So, how are you feeling now? Any better?"
> My daughter would reply with a question: "What do you mean?"
> Me: "Honey, I've been worried all day over your illness."
> Her: "Oh that? Oh, Mom, that was nothing. I'm fine."

The mother concluded:

> I knew, not only does a change need to occur, I'm the one who needs to make it. After all, my daughter wasn't concerned about it at all. She was texting all sorts of people throughout the day. I was merely one of them. So, when she returned home for Thanksgiving break, I said to her, "I love you, but we need to break up."

She looked at me with a mixed expression, part perplexed, part hurt. I went on to say, "This is not healthy for me, and it's not healthy for you. We can still talk on the phone, but I don't want to text you anymore."

The mother explained that this was an important step for both the daughter and herself. Her daughter's academic performance improved dramatically. She started getting help from academic counseling services offered by the college. Her grades improved. She realized that she also had some depression and ADD issues, and after several weeks of not texting and then getting help from the various services at the college, she called home and said, "All this time, I feel like I have been driving and not using the windshield wipers. Everything is so much clearer now, and I feel so much better about myself."

The mother told me,

> I'm not sure if we hadn't broken up she wouldn't still be in that slump. I had to get out of the way which forced her into a position where she had to take charge of her life, and just that simple act of stopping the texting seemed to make all the difference in the world. My daughter wound up graduating with a 3.8 GPA and had a wonderful summer internship which set her up for a great job after graduation.

This mother's story reminds us that cell phones aren't just for verbal conversations. In her book *The Big Disconnect: Protecting Childhood and Family Relationships in the Digital Age*, psychologist Catherine Steiner-Adair characterizes texting as "a conversation without tone or emotional complexity, content without substance. It is a shallow language of inference, not insight, and certainly not intimacy."[4] Word to the wise: While texting can be a good thing, this mother's story shows that it can also be too much of a good thing.

One More Rule: CELEBRATE!!!

A mother writes:

> I would add one more rule. Once you send your child off to college: CELEBRATE! This is a huge milestone for all involved.
>
> Once I had helped them unload the car and make umpteen trips up and down a small elevator to dump all that stuff in that seemingly tiny (but familiar-looking!) room, I didn't fuss or cry or make a scene. I pasted that cheery smile on my face and told each one how PROUD I was of them, how EXCITED I was for them at this great time of their lives, and what a WONDERFUL year they were going to have! And then I looked them straight in the eyes and quietly said to them in my "serious" mom voice: "Make. Good. Choices."
>
> Then I hugged them tight, told them I loved them, and left. No long farewells, no last minute "don't forgets." I just left.
>
> Then I cried in the car. Just a little bit.
>
> Each of my children has had a wonderful learning experience. Not perfect. Not without ups and downs, courses that didn't work out, professors who were a disappointment and even a broken heart or two. But they have all known that I am here (then, now, and forever) whenever they need advice or a shoulder or a hug. And I LOVE the role of consultant! When my kids went off to college, I didn't worry about them. I knew they were CAPABLE. And because I trusted them to handle their own lives, they didn't act like irresponsible children. That's not to say that they didn't make mistakes. We all do. But they are finding their respective paths.

Cringe-Worthy

A mother writes:

> Nothing makes me cringe more than to overhear a mom or dad at work on the phone "handling" an issue with a college-age son or daughter, or sharing with coworkers how they "have" to do this

or that for their grown child because, well, "he/she just won't do it if I don't." Please!!!

Cell Phones

The mother of four college graduates told me,

> We pay for their cell phones and we told them that we are committed to talk to each of them once per week. Sometimes it's more often, and occasionally it's less, but I'd say that it probably does work out to once per week per kid. It works well as far as maintaining a balance between keeping in touch while also providing enough space for every member of the family.

I talked with one mother who had sent three kids off to college, two in the pre–cell phone era and one in the era "when everyone had a phone." This mother observed,

> We did not pay for our son's cell phone when he was in high school. I think this led to a healthy relationship over the phone during his college years. I guess we sort of lucked into it. We just didn't think we should pay for his phone in high school, and it turned out that he appreciated our support in college.

Don't Fix . . . Ask Questions

Another mother of two college graduates concurs with this rule about calling, but she also warns that sometimes when your child calls it may be to request that you fix some problem they have, be it with a roommate, or a professor, or the food. To guard against this, she likes to respond with a question so when her son calls complaining about the roommate situation, she responds with, "Well, why don't you drop in on the Resident Advisor and discuss it with him?" Or, "Why not drop in on the professor and discuss the grade on the exam?" In other words, turn it back on your child.

The Critical First Two Weeks

The father of a Sacred Heart University student told me, "Everything I've heard and read says that the first two weeks are most critical for establishing both a strong start as well as the habits that will carry a student through the college experience. So, we tried to stay out of the picture."

Thus, he and his wife started out with a simple guideline: *We don't want to talk to you until you want to talk with us.*

Then after four days went by without a word from his daughter, he sent her a three-word text message: *Are you alive?* He remembers, "She called me after that, and I'd say that since then we've talked about once a week over the phone. I try to wait for her to initiate it."

He went on to say, "The choices are hers to make. The last time we spoke, she told me that she is thinking of dropping a course. I resisted the urge to comment on this decision. It's her call."

Choosing "Hands Off"

I heard from a father who told me a story suggesting that "who pays for what" can have deep ramifications for college success and beyond. This story could have been placed in Rules No. 1, No. 2, or No. 3 of this book as it speaks to all three. I'll let the father tell it himself:

> My wife and I went full circle after our son graduated from high school in 2008. He was accepted at Embry Riddle in Florida and although quite a distance, my parents lived in the area and I knew they would be a great support resource for our son. Luke had always wanted to fly, and given the school's national reputation for aviation study and preparation, this seemed to be the place for him.
>
> However, he did not make it to the November Thanksgiving break. He did not take his classes seriously, spent too much time working on a part-time job, and flunked out.

We chose to be hands off. It was hard as we had been told that things were going well, by both Luke and his grandparents whom he visited once a week. His dismissal was quite a shock.

Luke initially blamed his high school teachers. He blamed the college for not keeping tabs on him. He blamed the school for being too big. (Apparently missing the irony that the school had been his choice.) "Nobody cares," he said.

So, Luke returned home for a while. He announced his intention to work for a while and then attend another college the next fall, one that he maintained would be a better fit. After hearing him out, we informed him that he couldn't just hang around the house and wait for the next school year to roll around. We also presented him with a bill for $10,000: the cost of the semester that he had completely wasted.

Then in January he decided to go in another direction by enlisting in the air force where he did his four years, also earning an associate's degree in criminal justice. When he returned home he seemed to feel pretty good about himself, but despite his new degree, he did not want to pursue a career in law enforcement.

While his mother and I were wondering what might happen next, Luke went in yet another direction: He applied and earned admission to the Massachusetts School of Pharmacy. The great thing is that this decision is all on him. The cost will be paid by him and the GI bill. He did work this summer as a lifeguard and at a store in a local mall. There was a lot of anger on what happened and the wasted opportunities but we know he owns it.

This father also offered a few sound words of helpful advice to parents sending a child to college for the first time:

One thing I would suggest is for parents to visit their student a couple of months into the freshman year, especially if they are attending a college out-of-state. This might give a *real* sense of how your child is doing. After all, they tend to tell you what they want you to hear.

In closing, this father also observed,

My wife and I agree that the maturity level today of these college-bound kids is so far behind since we both attended college, worked part-time, graduated, and then went out into the business world . . . twenty-eight now seems to be the new eighteen and it is very sad.

On the one hand, this father may go too far for me. My experience tells me that kids are kids and that they don't change all that much from generation to generation. On the other hand, I indeed believe that the demarcation line between who is responsible for what in the American family has never been as blurred or broken as it is today and that this is due primarily to the tendency of today's parents to do too many things for their kids that they are actually completely capable of doing for themselves.

Wait to Hear from Them

One father said,

I have had kids at college and/or boarding schools for over nine years and I have never figured out a good time to call. They are either sleeping, in class, in the library (usually around exam time), or with friends. There is rarely a window for us to reach them, so we long ago gave up. Furthermore, we don't like to initiate a text or IM as we don't want to distract them from their work. We wait to hear from them and the waits can go on for a long time. I admit that many of the incoming calls are requests for help, usually monetary help. I may be wrong, but my memory of my college years is that I only called home once a week or less because long distance calls in those days were a luxury. We only had that one booth in the hallway in our dormitory and it was not very busy. I think it worked out OK.

The mother of two college students told me that she did indeed decide to "wait for their call." She explained,

We knew we had been deeply involved in our children's lives, and we saw college as the time for them to fly on their own. We are a close family and it was very hard not to call, but after a while we got into a rhythm where we spoke regularly but didn't cramp their style. I feel good about how my husband and I handled this part of our parenting while our children were away in college. Now that both are on their own, we talk regularly.

Try *Not* Taking Their Call

The mother of three college students said, "It took me three kids to learn." When I asked her to explain, she replied:

> When our first child headed off to NYU, we were so excited. Our child was moving more than one thousand miles east to live in the big city to attend this prestigious school, so we traveled east with him and made reservations to stay for five days to help him get situated. By Day Two, we began to pick up signs that we were becoming a nuisance to our son. By Day Three, he stopped answering his phone and simply said, "It's time for the two of you to go back home." (In what my interviews suggested was a reversal of roles, his dad called so much that the son simply shut off his phone.) We both left New York knowing that we had to change our approach.

The same mother told me that when she dropped her daughter off at the University of Colorado, her daughter called her on her cell phone thirteen times on the first day. (She remembers because she purposely kept track.) The calls were random and sometimes contradictory. At one point, she called to say how much she loved the school and her roommate, only to call a few hours later and announce that she now hated her roommate and wanted to find a new one.

By the third child this mother had learned to back off and avoid getting involved so much. She observed,

With the first two kids, I'd race to the phone and try to solve their problems. By the third one, I adopted a new rule that I think would be a very good one for parents to consider. It's simple—when they call, *don't* answer. Let it go to voice mail, hear what they've got to say, then maybe decide to call back or maybe not. In my case, I found, nine times out of ten, that our daughter was able to take care of whatever she had been dealing with at the time.

I would sometimes wait as long as twenty-four hours to call her back, and whether it was a roommate issue or fear of an upcoming exam, what I would invariably get from her when I did call was simply, "That's cool, Mom. I've worked it all out." With the first two kids, I would try to fix their problems; by the third one I basically stopped taking her call, and she was able to work out most of the things on her own. Not only did this free me up from getting over-involved in her issues, but it also helped build her confidence because she learned that she was quite capable of solving many, if not most, of her own problems.

This mother continued,

In the end, after three kids in college, I've learned two things. First, *I* have a life, and I need to begin to live it. Second, they can handle just about everything that comes up. These two lessons, once internalized and applied, have brought me a lot of peace of mind and have actually served the true long-term interests of my children.

Lessons from Sleep-Away Camp

One mother I spoke with observed that her experiences sending her son to a one-week summer sleep-away camp, nearly ten years before he was of college age, helped prepare both her and her son for college. He had never been away from home for a weekend to say nothing of a week. When she pulled up to the camp for Parent's Day, he greeted her with a hug and simple question: "Can I stay longer?" At the time, she thought, "Oh my God . . . he doesn't even want to see me!"

This same mother said that when her son was in college (2006–2010), "I bet we spoke four times. He was either too busy studying or working. He paid for everything so he had to work. So, we got caught up during his breaks."

Catch-as-Catch-Can

Echoing the comments of many parents I interviewed, the mother and father of four college students told me that communication with their children was mostly "catch-as-catch-can." Mom said,

> It was different with each kid. With one, I knew every grade she received on every test. With her brother, I never even knew what his GPA was. Incidentally, I was initially put off by the college's policy to leave the decision of who receives grade reports solely with the student. I couldn't fathom the idea that I could pay the whole bill and then be denied access to the grades. I decided to let it go. Hey, it's not my education.

Where's the Bread?

In interviewing parents for this book relative to "Wait for Their Call," I encountered a number of humorous anecdotes. However, truth be told, some of these revealed a level of over-engagement on the part of parents that made it a bit hard to laugh. For example, one mother told me about the mother of her child's friend. Apparently, this mother wrote the college an angry letter because her daughter was unable to find the bread in the cafeteria. This mother wanted the college to know that the bread should be placed in a more visible position in the cafeteria. One can only wonder why this mother did not insist that her daughter work this dilemma out on her own.

Let Me Tell You What's Going On with Me

The mother who told me the bread story noted that she and her husband tended to talk to their children once a week when they were in college, and they would always have part of the conversation embody a simple theme, "Let me tell you what's going on with me." Both parents and children would address this point. The mother observed that this kept these calls from being slanted one-way discussions where the child poured out all of his/her accomplishments or anxieties with the expectation that the parent would offer either praise or advice (or money). It made it more of a two-way conversation which, when you think about it, is what a conversation should be. (I mean . . . what a concept!)

"Whatever You Do . . . Turn Around"

The parents of three college graduates told me a story about the moment when they dropped their oldest one off for orientation at the University of Richmond. They had been carting various belongings back and forth between the parking lot and the dorm room and had reached the point where it was time to part ways. The son walked his parents down to the car. They hugged each other and the son turned and began walking back to his dorm, leaving his parents standing at the car. As they watched his back side walking away, "It felt as though he was walking out of our lives."

The mother said,

> I assumed he would turn around and offer a smile and a wave, but he just kept getting smaller as he moved away from us. I found myself getting anxious as I began to wonder if he was going to turn around at all. Next thing we knew, we watched him open the front door of the dormitory and disappear into the building. He was gone. I lost it. It just wasn't the way I had imagined it would all go down.

However, that's not the end of the story. As they were preparing to drive son number two to college, the father pulled him aside and gave him a wise piece of advice: "Whatever you do, when we say goodbye in the parking lot and you start walking back to the dorm, make sure, absolutely sure, that you turn around after a few strides and give your mom a good wave." Whereupon the son replied, "I'm way ahead of you, Dad. I know all about what happened with my brother. Don't worry, I got it covered."

NOTES

1. Hana Marano, *A Nation of Wimps: The High Cost of Invasive Parenting* (New York: Crown Archetype, 2008) , 179.

2. Ibid., 180.

3. Ibid., 189.

4. Catherine Steiner-Adair, *The Big Disconnect: Protecting Children and Family Relationships in the Digital Age* (New York: Harper Collins, 2013), 200.

Rule No. 3

STEP ASIDE

This isn't 13th grade. —Sacred Heart University administrator

I'll see you at Authorized Payer's Weekend. —The author, to a fellow college parent

Dude, quit telling your mom everything that happens here! — Notre Dame student to his roommate

My Take:

- Get Your Own Mentor

Parent Stories and Anecdotes:

- A Soccer Coach
- Coach #2
- Not Their Mentor
- Mock Trial Debate Coach
- "This Isn't 13th Grade"
- Dealing with Turkeys
- Change of Advisor
- Parental Access to Grades
- Introduction Leads to Job

- From Manager to Consultant
- Consultant #2
- Stepping Aside Pays Off . . . Years Later
- A Daughter Takes Charge of Her Own Psychological Well Being
- Step Aside . . . Before College
- Start Stepping Aside When Your Kids Are in High School
- A Daughter Argues for Herself
- A Daughter Designs Her Own Major
- Don't Decorate!
- Not Threats . . . but Partners
- OK, But How . . . Do I Step Aside?

MY TAKE

Get Your Own Mentor

If you are sending your child off to college, let's assume that you have been the primary mentor in your child's life for the past eighteen years. Let's also assume that you have done a good job. This rule asks you to consider the idea that it might not be a good idea for you to continue in the role of primary mentor in your child's life. It asks you, the parent, to step aside and allow new mentors to enter your child's life. College offers a wealth of fascinating and dynamic people who can make a huge difference in your child's life. It may be a professor; it may be a coach; it may be a work-study supervisor. Whoever it is, it should be someone . . . besides you. So, *step aside* and let it happen.

Years ago when I was in college, I set my sights on the lacrosse team. I found the coach to be an unrelenting task master, and went through a phase when I did not feel he was being fair regarding playing time—more specifically, *my* playing time. I even wondered that he might have been playing head games with me. I think I complained to my parents about this a couple of times, probably while sitting around the dinner table at home. I even got the sense that they might have agreed with me, but it would never have occurred to them to get involved.

Whatever was happening on that lacrosse team was *my* problem. Nearly four decades later, my relationship with that coach has been one of the most important ones in my personal and professional development. I count him as a friend and even dedicated the first book I wrote on college readiness (*Show Up, Study, & Serve: College Success Guaranteed* [Bath, ME: Unique Potential Press, 2010]) to him. Who knows what would have happened had my parents thrown themselves into the middle of the mix. For your child to get to where he/she is—about to enter college—you must have done something right. Now it's time to get out of the way and let all that good parenting you did take over as your child pursues and retains new mentors to take him or her to new heights.

One approach you might take is to get a mentor yourself and model the notion that one is never too old to get help from an accomplished person. In my case, I have taken up the harmonica, and my children have seen me work on this with far more talented musicians. While I'm doing this primarily in order to become a better harmonica player, it wouldn't be a bad thing if it served to encourage my children to take a similar approach with people who can help them accomplish new things.

PARENT STORIES AND ANECDOTES

A Soccer Coach

The mother of three college grads spoke of two roles that her son's soccer coach played in his life. First, she said, "He was unfair. And we thought that was good."

Observing my perplexed expression, she went on to explain,

> Our son was not getting very much playing time and he was convinced that his coach somehow "had it in for him." We didn't

know if that was true or not, but we thought that our son was dealing with a real life situation and that it was not our place to involve ourselves in it. After all, his playing time was none of our business. We felt for him, but it wasn't our problem.

The second role occurred near the end of her son's time at college. He was feeling very down due to a romantic break-up and uncertainty over his employment prospects after his upcoming graduation. Then one night, out of the blue, their phone rang at home and it was the coach on the other end of the line. He pointed out that he had noticed that her son seemed down in the dumps and he asked her if she thought it would be helpful if he had a word with him. Of course, she encouraged him to go ahead, which he did.

It turned out that the coach's words had a deep and positive impact on her son. The ironic thing is that she came to believe that her handling of the earlier issue regarding playing time served the purpose of allowing her son to establish a deep bond with his coach, one that resulted in him helping her son when he needed it most. The mom doubts that this would have happened had she intervened in the beginning.

Coach #2

The father of a Connecticut state university lacrosse player told me a story about how his son's coach became an important mentor in his life. After his junior season, Hank was involved in a fight in the town, one which resulted in police intervention. The coach had told all of his players that their character mattered as much to him as the quality of their play on the lacrosse field. The coach then lowered the boom. After requiring him to run laps throughout an entire practice, he benched Hank for the following game. He then told him that he would not be given consideration as captain of the team that year, a goal to which he had long aspired. The coach said, "You may not be able to be the captain, but you'll be given the chance to act as one."

The father resisted the urge to get involved, deciding to let the coach and Hank work it out together. When dad and coach finally did speak, the coach said, "Dad, you're raising a great kid. My job is to be here to help you do that." Indeed.

Not Their Mentor

The mother of three college graduates simply said, "I didn't consider myself their mentor when they were in college. I had completed that role and it was now up to them to find new mentors in their lives." Yup!

Mock Trial Debate Coach

The mother of a Dickinson College graduate told me that her son decided fairly early on that he wanted to study law after college. While both the mother and her husband are attorneys, and both were excited by their son's inclination, they wanted to stay out of his way and permit him to consider his life's options on his own. They definitely felt it was important for their son to connect with new mentors. Enter a mock trial debate coach. Although their son had participated in debating in high school, his debate coach at the college helped him reach new heights with his sense of presence, delivery, and skills. He also interacted with the college president in this regard. Furthermore, he made lasting relationships with older students who were also interested in the law. Most important: he arranged all of these opportunities for himself, and he knows he did. These experiences obviously paid off for him as today he attends an Ivy League law school.

"This Isn't 13th Grade"

The father of a Sacred Heart University student recounted something that university administrators had said to the parents of all first-year students at the close of new student orientation: "This isn't 13th grade."

Presumably, the intent was to jar parents out of the high school mindset and move them to a more hands-off demeanor. While this father didn't seem to require such jarring, the point obviously left an impression.

Dealing with Turkeys

The Sacred Heart father also noted that his daughter's experiences with her high school swimming and softball coaches helped him learn to step aside. It also helped his daughter learn to work out more of her problems on her own. One time in high school, she came home with tales of woe about the shortcomings of one of her coaches. Her father said to her, "You may think he's a turkey. Hey, you might even be right, but sometime in your life you will undoubtedly work for a turkey. Just think of the training you're getting right now!" She worked it out.

Change of Advisor

The mother of a Providence College student told me that her daughter wasn't getting what she needed out of her advisor:

> When she called home, I was able to give some objective advice—a simple suggestion that she consider getting a new academic advisor—but I refrained from jumping in to try to fix the problem. My daughter was contemplating a change in major, which she ultimately decided to do, and this led her to a different group of faculty members, and she wound up with a new advisor. Not only did this new advisor meet her needs, my daughter had gained confidence by realizing that she was capable of making this advisor change which, in turn, bolstered her own confidence. Ironically, I helped her out by making a simple suggestion and then . . . doing nothing.

Parental Access to Grades

More than a few parents complained about the now common practice of requiring permission from the student before grades can be shared with parents. One joked, "It's like the college says, 'I can't show you your kid's grades, but I do need to tell you that it's time for you to send another tuition check.'"

Having made friends with some of my daughter's parents at her college, I once said to one, "I'll see you at Authorized Payer's Weekend." (That's the salutation at the top of the letter when the bill comes.) For what it's worth, I can understand this policy to some extent, perhaps as a symbolic gesture, but given the fact that the overwhelming majority of college bills are paid primarily by parents, I can't shake the feeling that the practice smacks a bit of "playing house." (Now, in those cases where the student actually is paying all or part of the bill, I take it all back!)

In any case, the father of a Sacred Heart University student has an interesting approach to this issue. His daughter has been enrolled in a seven-year bachelor's/graduate program that requires a minimum GPA of 3.2. Hence, he told his daughter, "I do not intend to interfere with your college affairs, but if you dip below a 3.2, I'm definitely gonna get involved. I'm committed to serving as the 'payer,' but I will expect proof that you're holding up your end of the arrangement."

Introduction Leads to Job

If you remember the story of the UMaine mother whose son paid his own way through school, it may not surprise you that her son's initiative extended beyond paying for college. During his internship with one of the major rental car companies, the CEO came to visit campus. Her son thought to himself, "I want him to know my name. I want him to know my face." So, he made it a point to introduce himself. He also noticed that none of his peers made the same move. (Note: Today he has a full-time job with the same company!)

While in school, this same young man also had a job with the local Sears department store, where he had a supervisor who impressed upon him the idea that no matter your job status or duties, the work ethic is all that matters. Today, whenever he is told that he has a great work ethic, he tells people that he learned it from a sales worker in the appliance section at Sears. (Some people *never* learn it!) Both jobs were earned due solely to his own initiative, his mother stepping aside throughout.

From Manager to Consultant

The father of a University of Vermont student was delighted when his son decided to major in economics. The father was at the peak of a successful career in investment banking and was delighted to observe his son following in his footsteps. However, he resisted the urge to give any advice to his son or to badger him about what he was learning or question the emphases the various finance professors were taking with his son's program. He was surprised to receive a big pay-off during his son's junior year when his son began to call him and ask his advice. Assigned to write a paper on financial investing, he called his father and they shared a discussion that was particularly meaningful to the father.

The father's story reminded me of the Pursuer-Distancer Dynamic described in the "Rule No. 2: Wait for Their Call" chapter. By the father holding his tongue, the son found his way back to him and they shared very meaningful discussions about economics. The father was certain these discussions would not have occurred had he set about to badger his son.

Consultant #2

A mother notes,

> Our second child went off to Miami University of Ohio where she eagerly took on the challenges of a very demanding science

curriculum. She initially signed up for one of the hardest courses in the department and from the get-go, our daughter saw that she was pretty far over her head. She soldiered on for the first few weeks before concluding that she needed to spend more time in more introductory courses before tackling such an advanced class. She also felt that the course simply wasn't for her, feeling that she misunderstood the emphasis of the course. Distraught over her predicament, she called home.

When she called home to ask our advice, everything in me wanted to console her and somehow "fix" this problem for her. However, choosing her long-term interests over her short-term comfort, I steeled myself and told her that there was nothing I could do. Trying to be helpful, but from a distance, I suggested that she go see the department chair.

Lo and behold, our daughter followed my advice. She had a discussion with the department chair who helped her switch to another course. Had this class change occurred earlier in the semester, this would have been an easy transition, but classes were well under way, and our daughter had to face the challenge of catching up in a course that had already been operating for a few weeks. She took it upon herself to get some tutorial help from a professor recommended by the department chair. She made up the work she had missed and forged ahead. Not only did she catch up, she wound up getting an A in the course!

This mother told me that it took everything in her to resist the temptation to call the college and get involved. Instead, she stepped aside and allowed her daughter to handle the whole affair. While it was wonderful that it all worked out for the best with a grade of A in the course, it was an even better thing that this daughter learned that she could handle her own responsibilities, advocate for herself, and manage her life.

Stepping Aside Pays Off . . . Years Later

When he learned of my work on this book, the father of a former student shared this inspirational story, a testament to stepping aside. The father writes:

> My son left high school after four up-and-down years. At the time I thought he should have been a little bit better prepared but now I am willing to concede that maybe his teachers did the best with what they had to work with.
>
> Anyway, Tad got early acceptance from a college that had a reputation as a party school. He enrolled, roomed with a buddy from high school, and was a happy camper who discovered fraternity beer parties. But after one semester, Tad had only earned one credit. (And had a disciplinary record with the folks over at campus security!) My wife and I talked it over and decided not to negotiate with him over continuing. I just said, "You're out of there, buddy. We'll let you live at home for a few months while you decide how to earn a living. I'm not wasting any more of my money." Frankly, I think he was relieved. He was not ready for college life.
>
> He got a job waiting tables and after a bit of this, his boss recommended him to one of his friends who was a beer distributor and needed someone strong in the warehouse. He did well there and they helped him to get his Class A commercial driver's license. Soon he was driving one of those big beer trucks and making good money. He said, "Wow, I'm only 19 years old and I'm making $39,000 per year. This is pretty good."
>
> His mother and I looked at each other and then up at the ceiling.
>
> After a few months, he got a speeding ticket and was put on probation. I mentioned that this was not good behavior for a professional driver. Then he heard of another outfit that paid their beer drivers $54,000 and he got greedy. He talked with them and said they offered him a job; so he gave his two-week notice to the first firm. But after ten days he had not heard from the second. So, he called and they told him, "Yeah, we talked but we never offered you a job. We don't have any openings right

now." And then, as luck might have it, the first firm said he could not return, and he would be off the rolls in three days; they had already hired another fellow to fill in behind him. This taught my son one of life's tough lessons: a bird in the hand is worth two in the bush.

Several weeks passed and one night he said, "Maybe I just ought to go into the Service and get my life squared away. His mother and I looked at each other and tried not to break out in grins and high fives.

So, I said I thought it was a good idea. It took almost a year before he was able to report to boot camp. He became a good Marine, serving three-and-a-half years as a combat engineer with two tours in Afghanistan. He came out early to restart college.

He now lives in our basement and is going to the local community college on the GI Bill. His first semester he got a 3.75. He was selected by the athletic coach to be co-captain of the lacrosse team and is very motivated to perform well in that position. He plans to move on after his associate degree and get his bachelor's in electrical engineering. Then he plans to use his security clearance and veteran status to help him get a job in the government.

He has become a mature young man of twenty-five with life goals and a plan. He says, "Once a Marine, Always a Marine." He has turned out just fine. His parents are immensely proud of him.

Me too.

A Daughter Takes Charge of Her Own Psychological Well Being

The mother of a Providence College student told me a story of how her daughter took the initiative to address some personal issues in her life.

My daughter was basically a student who did not meet her academic potential at a high-achieving high school. She had always had some issues with anxiety; we knew that. While we all sensed that there may have been some ADD issues involved, we also felt she was being dramatic, that she would grow out of it if we just continued to manage and control everything for her— that was my job as mom, or so I felt! Right or wrong, her high school career wrapped up on a strong note and everything turned out OK, which meant that she got into the school of her "stretch" choice, Providence College.

Her freshman year there was a "stinker." She had a court date for underage drinking, and her GPA took a huge hit for violating the school's plagiarism policy. My husband and I (maybe more me) spent time trying to manage her from afar.

Our daughter showed courage when she quietly went for personal help without telling us. (Why would she tell us? We told her she was fine!) She started at Academic Services, moved on to the school's Counseling Center, and ended up in a psychiatrist's office in Providence near Brown University.

After hearing her story, the psychiatrist immediately put her on ADD meds. Maybe it took us letting go for her to realize that she was fully capable of asking for help herself. She was diagnosed with ADD-inattentive, manages her own medication, and today takes justifiable pride in the academic success she has had at Providence.

This mother's story suggests that sometimes you have to know when *not* to get involved in your children's challenges.

Step Aside . . . Before College

When it comes to stepping aside, nearly all my interviews affirmed one important point: Stepping aside is hard to do cold turkey. It's easier to do at the college drop-off if you've been practicing it all along.

I remember back in high school art class when we were studying Asian art and my teacher said something to the effect of, "The essence of Japanese art has less to do with what is added than with what is left out." The same is often true with parenting.

When a teaching colleague told me about his son's and daughter's perhaps unconventional path to fulfillment and success, I was reminded of that observation about Japanese art.

I moved Jim to Miami when he was a junior in high school and enrolled him at the school where I was teaching. He was unhappy about leaving his old school and felt like a fish out of water at his new school. His lack of motivation caused a degree of self-destruction with a string of Ds and Fs. After his junior year, there was a discussion about repeating his junior year. Instead, he chose to take and pass his GED and enroll at Miami Dade Community College (now a full four-year college). He also worked a part-time job to pay for his expenses.

He loved his course work, small classes, and more mature setting for learning. At the same time, as a result of completing a summer pre-college art program in Sarasota, as he is artistically talented, he became riveted on film. Jim began to explore college programs with film as a major. He ended up discovering an alternative program at Full Sail in Orlando, Florida, enrolled, and completed an associate's degree in film. He had the option of completing the BA film program, which included more of the business side of the industry, but did not want to assume any more tuition debt at the time.

The positive about this development is that he was honoring a genuine passion. The film industry is not one to enter just as a result of what school you graduate from. It is a hard road. Jim has written and filmed an independent short film, and more specifically, discovered that he loved and was talented at writing film scripts. On his own he has become a self-educated expert on film genres and history. Currently he is a marketing director at a high-end dinner-movie theater in south Florida that runs top releases as well as international opera, concert, and independent films. This is a step along his career path that started with his decision for post-high school education.

My friend then described his daughter's higher education experience. Perhaps not surprisingly, she had a similar trajectory:

Dorothy was an A-B student in high school, and her extracurricular activities involved dance and horseback riding. She attended the independent day school where I taught (from seventh through tenth grade) and we all loved both the small classes as well as the personalized challenge of this educational environment. When we moved to Tampa, where I was to develop a high school division at a PK–8 independent school, Dorothy chose to attend a local (huge) public school.

This new school was foreign territory for her, but she was self-motivated and self-directed and made it work for her. However, upon graduation from high school, she felt more comfortable in starting her college career at a community college—which she enjoyed and appreciated as a result of the small classes and mature educational setting. Although artistically talented, Dorothy was not comfortable with majoring in art as she saw being creative as part of a life-style versus a career emphasis at the time. She eventually fell in love with history and culture, and then decided to go into the study of anthropology, and minoring in art.

She transferred to the University of South Florida in Tampa, a school with a large and diverse anthropology department. She thrived. (Note: Dorothy was eligible for a 75 percent tuition break when attending a Florida college or university as a result of her high school GPA, SAT scores, and service hours.) She did apply for financial aid and grants to help with expenses. The culmination of her college experience, which included a part-time job at a museum in Tampa, was to mix her career interests in both art and museum work. She is now taking some postgraduate course work in graphic arts in order to support her career goals and attain the skills she will need to be hired. About to complete all her course work from this art institute in Tampa, she is working a part-time job to be able to support herself.

While I am delighted by the success that the above Florida brother and sister experienced during their college years, from my standpoint, a big factor in the success of both has to do with what the father (and mother) did . . . and did *not* do during the process.

Start Stepping Aside When Your Kids Are in High School

The mother of four college graduates told me, "We started stepping aside when our kids were in high school. One time when our daughter was kicked out of her senior government class (for being late to class with what seemed to us a legitimate excuse), we simply said, 'It's between you and Mr. Blank.'"

This mother and father figured that their daughter could handle this situation on her own. They were right. And she did.

The mother also observed that she had no idea that the situation also helped prepare her to be a better parent to her college-age children.

Similarly, the mother of an NYU student told me that she was thankful that her son had developed the ability to seek and nurture mentoring relations while in high school. He had a deep interest in studying Spanish and was fortunate enough to connect with a teacher who helped him rise to a level of advanced Spanish, where he took his final course one-on-one with his teacher. He developed this relationship on his own, and it stood him in good stead for making the transition to college.

A Daughter Argues for Herself

It would be fair to count me among those who believe that our colleges today could do a better job presenting and teaching a more balanced view of conservative versus liberal political philosophies. (Full Disclosure: I am an Independent.)

As the 2012 presidential election geared up, one of my daughters was struggling mightily with the fact that she felt out-numbered and out-gunned. As she said, "Dad, anyone in the class who even hints at sympathizing with any Republican sensibilities just gets savaged by the whole class. I can't recall ever encountering such close-minded people. I think I'm the only one who takes them on."

The whole thing made my blood boil. I said to my wife, "How can any place that professes such a deep commitment to diversity have so little regard for diversity of thought?" I didn't say or do anything about it, but it indeed bugged me.

At the end of the semester, my daughter was very proud of the "A" she received in the class. She told me that her professor made a point of pulling her aside and thanking her for so passionately and articulately arguing the minority opinion during class discussions. He said something to the effect of, "Without you, class sessions might have been pretty boring."

The whole experience turned out to be one of the most meaningful ones of my daughter's college career. Glad I didn't intervene and ruin it!

A Daughter Designs Her Own Major

The parents of an Elon University student told me about their daughter's experience designing and arguing in support of her own major. The mother said:

> After designing the major, she was expected to recruit three professors who would stand in support of her major. She went out and spoke to the professors and ultimately made it happen. While she never asked her father or me to help her with this, I suspect she knew that we would have simply turned it back to her and wished her well. In any case, the whole experience from design, to recruiting the professors, to defending the design in front of the "powers that be" was a true highlight of her college education.

Kudos to Mom and Dad for stepping aside!

Don't Decorate!

At the conclusion of one of my interviews, one mother said, "And one more thing: Let your kids decorate their own dorm rooms however they want to! Stay out of it, Mom!"

She went on to explain, "When I dropped my son off at Notre Dame, it was tough to watch his roommate's mom step in and try to take charge of what the room would look like . . . 'Put that poster here; the desk lamp doesn't belong there,' etc."

Apparently, the mom's failure to step aside didn't end with decorating tips: "In the early going, this mom and her son talked every night. After it negatively impacted my son's ability to get a good night's sleep, my son finally said to his roommate, 'Dude, quit telling your Mom everything that happens here.' The good news is that the roomie heeded my son's advice and things got better from there."

Not Threats . . . but Partners

The mother of two college graduates said,

> I deeply wanted my children to have as deep an experience as possible, one fueled by a wide range of influences. From the beginning, I tried to consciously remind myself that the new mentors entering their lives were not threats to me, but rather, were *partners* in my parenting. How else could my children develop new talents and new directions for their future lives? Were there times when I might have felt a tad jealous?—Sure, but I could also see the difference these people were having in their lives, and I was glad for that. Even the bad influences played a role. After all, maybe you can't really appreciate the good if you haven't had some bad, and learned how to sort out the difference.

The mother of a St. Lawrence University student told me of the mentoring relationship her son experienced while serving as a summer intern for a Wall Street commodities broker. She said:

> This guy went way beyond teaching our son the basics of the commodities world. Sure, he taught him about the business, but more importantly, he taught him about life. He taught him how to dress, proper manners, how to interact with others, basically

how to act while out on the floor. The funny thing is that he also could have learned a lot of this stuff from his father and other relatives who are familiar with the workings of Wall Street. But the fact that it was a stranger worked better. It was easier for my son to listen to him.

When I asked if she or her husband felt threatened by this relationship, she replied, "Not in the least. We were grateful to have another teammate join in our common cause."

OK, But How . . . Do I Step Aside?

At an organization called Growing Leaders, Tim Elmore helps to serve NCAA and professional sports teams. In a recent blog post, he seems to be borrowing from Michael Riera's playbook (see http://growingleaders.com/blog/what-parents-should-say-as-their-kids-perform/#sthash.Ko4BTrQ8.dpuf):

> After meeting with hundreds of coaches and athletes, I noticed an issue kept surfacing in our conversations. Both the student-athlete and the coach were trying to solve the same problem. What was that problem?
>
> The parents of the student-athletes.
>
> You may or may not believe this, but even in Division One athletics, parents stay engaged with their child's sport, often at the same level they did through their growing-up years. Moms will call coaches and advise them on how to encourage their daughter or son. Dads will call coaches and ask why their kid isn't getting more playing time. Parents will call strength and conditioning coaches and inquire what they're doing about their child's torn ligament. Each of these calls is understandable. After all, no one has more at stake than the parent of a performer. They love their child, they've invested in their child and they want to see a "return on their investment." Some athletes refer to their moms as their P.A. (personal assistant) or their agent. I know a mother who watches her collegiate daughter's gymnastics practice behind the glass, all the while, calling and leaving

voicemails for the coach on what should be done for her little girl. I even know sets of parents who moved into a condo across the street from their freshman athlete's university. They didn't want to miss a thing, and they certainly didn't want to neglect to provide direction. I understand this. I am a father of two kids myself.

What we parents may not recognize is the pressure and angst this kind of involvement implies. May I tell you what student-athletes are telling me?

1. I love my mom, but when she does this, I get the feeling she doesn't trust me.
2. My parents are great, but I feel like I have multiple coaches telling me what to do and I get stressed out over it.
3. I'm getting blackballed by my teammates because my mother keeps texting me and my coach, to give suggestions. I wish she would chill.
4. I feel like I'm never quite good enough; I can never fully please my parents.

Moving From Supervisor to Consultant

According to years of research on athletes, I believe parents have a more productive impact on their kids by making a change in their style. When our kids were younger, we played the role of supervisor. We were right there on top of the issues. And we should be—they were young and needed our support. As they age, parents must move to the role of consultant. We're still involved, still supportive, but we allow our kids to grow up and self-regulate. When we fail to do this—we can actually stunt their growth. It's a bit like teaching our kids to ride a bike. Remember this process? First, we gave them a tricycle. The three wheels made it almost impossible for them to fall off, and they got used to pedaling a vehicle. Then, they moved to a bicycle. It was bigger and had only two wheels. A little more scary. So we initiated them on that bike with training wheels. That prevented bad accidents. Eventually, however, we took the training wheels off, and our involvement became a tender balance of two ingredients: support and letting go. Did you catch that? Support and letting go.

Later in the same post, Elmore goes so far as to offer a script of what parents might say both before and after their children compete in athletic competition.

What We Should Say When Our Kids Perform

The most liberating words parents can speak to their student-athletes are quite simple. Based on psychological research, the three healthiest statements moms and dads can make as they perform are:

Before the competition. After the competition:

1. Have fun. 1. Did you have fun?

2. Play hard. 2. I'm proud of you.

3. I love you. 3. I love you.

Rule No. 4

MANTRA: IS THIS MY ISSUE?

First, why don't you give it more time. Second, maybe you should find a beer you like. —Mother to her college son after a tough first semester

You're one bad decision away from ruining your life. —Father dropping his daughter off at college

Fair or unfair, it was something my daughter needed to work out on her own. —Mother whose daughter had just flunked a course

My Take:

- Obstacles as Opportunities
- Pendulum Swinging
- The Difficulty of Allowing Our Children to Struggle

Parent Anecdotes and Stories:

- Boyfriend: 3's Company
- Our Daughter Takes Charge
- When in Doubt: Don't Fix
- When Your Child Chooses the Wrong School
- The Kitchen Is a Pig Sty!

- One Bad Decision Away
- College Laundry: True Story
- When He/She Flunks Out: A Mother's Story
- When the College Falls Short
- Roommate Issues—Six Stories
- Disciplinary Trouble at School
- Wanting to Call the College
- Wanting to Call . . . Even More!
- When It *Is* Your Issue
- You and Your Spouse Don't Have to Agree
- A Daughter Advocates For and Receives a Merit Scholarship
- Professor Problems
- A Mother Asks for Help
- If there Is an Issue . . . Who Owns It?
- The Value of Doing It Wrong
- Life Is an "And" . . . Not an "Or"

MY TAKE

Rule No. 4 is actually a mantra for parents to internalize when they are engaged in communications with their college child. Should a call come in from an exasperated son or daughter regarding an incident involving a roommate, a professor, the food, the dormitory, or the weather, stop and ask yourself, "*Is this my issue?*"

However, to take it one step further, before you respond with your "final answer," try "No" on for size. In other words, give "No" serious consideration as your "go to" answer. You may ultimately decide that "Yes" is the proper answer, and sometimes it is . . . sometimes.

Obstacles as Opportunities

In our book *The Biggest Job We'll Ever Have*, my wife, Laura, and I present ten priorities designed to help parents build better families.

One of these, Priority No. 6, is called *Allow Obstacles to Become Opportunities*. At the workshops we present, we play an association game where we ask parents to blurt out words that spring to mind when they hear the word "obstacle." Typical responses are: "problem" . . . "something to fix" . . . "barrier" . . . "hurdle" . . . "embarrassment" . . . "get over."

Then we ask participants to do the same for the word "opportunity." Typical responses for that word are: "vision" . . . "positive" . . . "something good" . . . "growth" . . . "potential advantage."

What a difference! This priority is about letting go of the myth that problems are a sign of weakness and realizing that obstacles come as a result of high expectations. The more you strive to accomplish, the more you will be asked to struggle. Just think what might happen if we chose to attach some of the above words associated with opportunity and applied them to our obstacles!

Pendulum Swinging

Many parents I encounter in my work are overly engaged in their children's trials and tribulations, especially compared with the parents I worked with when I began teaching in the 1970s. As I have suggested earlier in this book, I fear that the parents of today's high school kids have swung the pendulum too far to the side of parental over-engagement. The example of attending all athletic contests (and some practices) has been mentioned. I have observed that parents who resent the idea that their own parents never shared their emotions will try to over-compensate by sharing theirs in overdrive. If they feel that their parents were overly strict, they might be decidedly lenient in terms of enforcing rules and standards. More than a few times I have felt that some parents are trying to fix their family of origin, a futile effort if there ever was one.

So when your child calls you and complains about his/her roommate's grooming habits, a grade-stingy professor, the food, a lumpy mattress, a coach who doesn't give him/her much playing time, ask the question: "Is this my issue?" (Hint: All of those would get a clear "No.") Furthermore, I recommend that you go one step more and intentionally try "No" on for size as your initial response.

The question can serve as a simple check and balance on your parenting. I do not suggest that your intervention is never warranted, only that without this mantra, your natural instinct might lead you into inserting yourself into any number of circumstances that your child is perfectly capable of addressing on his or her own. (And that might include bringing in someone to help . . . *besides* you.) The bottom line: These days I rarely encounter under-involved parents. (In fact, it's almost refreshing whenever I do!)

Another point to consider is the message we give our kids, albeit unintentionally, when we step in and fix things for them. In exchange for our own (and their) short-term good feelings and peace of mind, we run the risk of communicating a message to them that says, "We love you, but we doubt that you could have ever worked this problem out on your own. So, we went ahead and fixed it for you." There's really no way to tell what impact this message might have on their confidence.

The Difficulty of Allowing Our Children to Struggle

In midcoast Maine where I live, there was an incident a few years ago that had TV stations, newspapers, and Internet message boards buzzing involving a high school student-athlete found to be in violation of her school's athletic honor code. After photos of her holding a beer can were posted on Facebook, she wound up being suspended from the team for three weeks. Her parents wound up taking the matter to the courts where a federal judge ultimately refused to grant an injunction that would have allowed her to play.

Consequently, editorial and Internet chat rooms lit up with opinions flaring on honor codes, student discipline, moral decline, good/bad parenting, and the like.

The actions of the girl's parents reflected a current reality: *We parents of current teenagers have a very difficult time allowing our children to struggle.* Hence, we want to plow the path in front of them to ensure that they will either not have failures or will recover quickly from them. In *A Nation of Wimps*, Hara Marano observes that even the "Helicopter Parent" has become passé, having been replaced by the "Snowplow Parent."

At the same time, our better selves know that struggles and failures are where all of us learn the most. Perhaps you have heard the fable of the man walking in the woods who comes across a caterpillar struggling to fight out of a cocoon. Perceiving the caterpillar to be engaged in futile effort, he reaches up and snips the cocoon with a pair of scissors, thereby "freeing" the caterpillar. The caterpillar then plummets to the earth and dies shortly thereafter. The man did not realize that Mother Nature has designed an intentional process whereupon the caterpillar must struggle in the cocoon in order to develop sufficient muscles to allow its wings to fly its body away as a butterfly. Interference with this process can result in serious long-term damage. As the TV commercial from days of old warned, "It's *not* nice to fool with Mother Nature!"

Rather than jump in to rescue our kids from their difficulties, all of us will do well to ask a very simple question: Is this really *my* issue? In the case of the honor code and the girl with the beer can, both the parents and the students had signed an honor code and the student had plainly broken the code. I am not a big fan of honor codes. I also believe that we, as a culture, truly lost something when we took the authority out of the hands of individual coaches and transferred it over to the school to make blanket rules. Having been a coach for a long time myself, I see these matters as between the player and the coach. It is the parent's role to spectate, and spectate only. At least, that's the way things should be.

This incident also reminds me of a story from my own youth that illustrates the extent to which things have changed. In the sixth grade, I had been verbally disrespectful to the substitute teacher. She also caught me chewing gum in class, a big "no-no" back in the day. The following day, my teacher (who happened to be the principal of the school) returned. Adopting a somber tone, he addressed the class: "I understand we had some problems yesterday. Malcolm, please come forward."

I did as instructed and was then asked to hold out my hand which he proceeded to whack three times with a heavy eighteen-inch wooden ruler. Then he pulled out a small tin case, produced a piece of Ivory Soap, and demanded that I chew it. I deposited the soap in my mouth, chomped on it for maybe fifteen seconds—it felt like an hour!—and burst out of the room and spent fifteen minutes at the water fountain rinsing my mouth out.

While I can't say that either penalty caused me any lasting damage, both were excessive and would be grounds for a firing today in any Maine school district. (Imagine how today's chat rooms would light up over that one!) However, that's not my point.

I came home after school that day and did not tell my parents what had happened. I did not want them to find out because I was fully aware of the fact that, in our house, trouble at school meant double trouble at home. A few days passed and then my mother stopped me and said, "Malcolm, I just heard an amazing story. Somebody told me that you were caught chewing gum . . . that you were also insubordinate to the substitute teacher . . . and that you were then whacked with a ruler and then forced to chew part of a bar of soap. Is that true?!?"

Sensing some sympathy from my mother, I boldly replied, "Yeah, it's true, all right!" She then stated her belief that I had been subjected to an extremely harsh penalty, one that was not at all fair. I nodded in agreement. Then she asked, "Tell me, did you know that that was the penalty for chewing gum in class?" I said, "Yes, I did." She paused, and then said, "Oh." She followed this with a warning about tempting fate. She walked off, and we never discussed it again. If she contacted the school, she never mentioned it and I never inquired.

To be sure, my mother was Old School. Nearly a half-century later I would not necessarily say that I agree with the approach she took regarding that incident. However, her message on that day was clear and simple: *If you want to dance, you've got to pay the fiddler. So, if you don't want to pay, don't dance.*

I doubt that there is one parent in a thousand who would act today as my mother did back in 1966. But rather than get caught up in guessing what you might do in the same circumstance, just continue to ask that question: Is this *my* issue? If the answer is "No," then step aside and let your child fight through the difficulties. Trust that Mother Nature has a plan in mind. You can help, but don't interfere.

In the remainder of this chapter, you will undoubtedly see that the stories told by parents of current college students and recent graduates fall into one of three categories:

We did X and we are glad we did;
We did X and we wish we didn't;
We wish we had done X, but we failed to act.

I confess that while our kids were in college, my wife and I made decisions and carried out actions that would fit in all three categories.

PARENT ANECDOTES AND STORIES

Boyfriend: 3's Company

The mother of a Clark University (Massachusetts) student was deeply troubled when she learned that her daughter's roommate had a boyfriend, a student at another university, who was a frequent overnight guest. Not only did this add up to a lot of nights where her daughter was either finding another place to sleep or would be placed in an uncomfortable circumstance by staying in her own room, it triggered deep anxiety in the mother. The mother told me,

> I just knew that I could clear the path so well for her on this. . . .
> My blood was boiling. In fact, words cannot convey the depth
> and breadth of the issues that I had with this. But . . . is it *my*
> issue?
>
> The fact that my daughter told me that this was going on
> suggests that she has a problem with it as well. But it is her issue,
> not mine. Believe me, I thought to call the school, the RA, the

mother of the roommate, even the mother of the boyfriend. But it is my daughter's battle to wage and I have held my tongue, except to say to her that I believe she is being taken advantage of. She did not like that.

I must say that I give this mother a lot of props for her handling of this. She is letting her daughter handle it, but she is also being true to herself by openly telling her daughter how she feels about it. As parents, that's all we can do.

Our Daughter Takes Charge

Our older daughter excelled in high school in the classroom and on the athletic field. Early in her senior year she decided to apply Early Decision to one of the most selective liberal arts colleges in the country. She, her family, and her teachers thought her chances were good. In addition to her strong grades and athletic honors, she could check the proverbial legacy box given that three previous generations of family members had attended the school, not to mention some aunts and uncles. Then the decision letter arrived in her mail box. It was thin. And it began with "We regret to inform you . . . "

She was crushed. So were her teachers and family members. As a parent, it hurt to see her so bummed out. My wife took the lead. She said simply, "Honey, we love you. Let us know if we can help. But I want you to know that we believe in you and we know that you will rise above the way you feel and will wind up in a great college situation."

The previous summer I had taken both my daughters on a couple of college tours where we logged a few thousand miles on our car. I had liked a number of the schools and figured that my daughter would wind up at one of the schools we visited. Then one day, after she had accepted and come to terms with her rejection from her first choice, she said to me, "Dad, there's one more school I want to see—the University of Denver—and I'd like to go check it out by myself." Her mother and I agreed to cover the travel costs and away she went, two thousand miles from our home in Maine, to take a look.

She returned from her long weekend with a simple announcement: "I could really see myself at that school." She was admitted and given a substantial merit scholarship. She went on to spend four years there, studied hard (earning a 3.5 GPA), played hard, skied a lot, and made a number of lifelong friends. Her program included a semester in London as well as a summer internship at an executive search firm in Philadelphia that ultimately hired her out of college. She works there today.

The point of this story is that our daughter ultimately took charge of her circumstances and created better ones for herself. Not only did she have a wonderful college experience, she knows that she had the biggest hand in making it happen. I could not put a price on that feeling.

When in Doubt: Don't Fix

A mother of two college graduates told me that she has long asked the question tied to this mantra and has found more often than not that her children have been able to figure their way out of most of the challenges they face, including many that she did not think they could handle. She told me, "If I could say one thing to parents with a kid going off to college, I'd say, 'Don't be a fixer.' When we parents jump in to fix our kids' problems, sometimes the cure can be worse than the disease. While you might fix a short-term problem, you might also be feeding a negative long-term tendency. To take it out another step, you might even consider this notion: When in doubt, don't!"

The mother of a Dickinson College graduate reflected this sentiment when her freshman son came home at Thanksgiving with a long list of things he didn't like about the school. While he had few complaints about his classes and his academic performance seemed to be strong, he went on and on about the social side, particularly about the fraternity he had joined and "some frat guy who controls everything we do for fun."

The mother calmly took it all in and made two simple suggestions: "First, why don't you give it more time. Second, maybe you should find a beer you like."

That was it. The next break, their son had few complaints. Three and a half years later he graduated and today attends law school. Sometimes doing nothing is the best move. In fact, when it involves your kid at college, it's probably the right move.

This story also suggests another consideration during trying times: Sometimes time itself is a very effective remedy.

When Your Child Chooses the Wrong School

The mother of a daughter enrolled at a respected Midwestern college told me her daughter called her a few weeks into the semester and said, "I know I've made a mistake in my choice of school." She continued, "It is an excellent college but just not the one for me. My roommate and I are not getting along at all, and this simply makes matters worse. I know you want me to stay for the full year before I decide, but I just don't think this is for me."

After the mother made a few attempts to get her daughter to consider staying on for that full first year, she decided to take a different tack. "You either need to be in school or get a job," she said to her daughter. "We are not going to make you return for the second semester, but you're also not going to come home and laze around while you are thinking about your next move. So you need to get a job, and you need to do the college search yourself."

The daughter came home, got a job, researched her college choices, spoke with her old high school college counselor, reconsidered some of the other colleges she had looked at a year before, and wound up enrolling at the Fashion Institute of Technology (FIT) that January. Three and a half years later she graduated from FIT . . . *magna cum laude.*

As the mother concluded,

If I had been able to have my way, I would have talked her into at least finishing that first year at the first school. However, the way things worked out proved that she knew best, and her father and I never stepped in to "fix" her predicament. She handled it all on her own which has turned out to be a valuable life lesson for a lot of aspects of her life since college.

The Kitchen Is a Pig Sty!

The father of a first semester college student told me that he was irked by the condition of the kitchen across the hall from his daughter's dormitory room. Given how much he was paying in tuition dollars, it just didn't seem right. "It was a pig sty," he told me. Then, just as he was planning to call the dean about it, the "Is This *My* Issue?" mantra kicked in. He concluded, "It's my daughter's problem. She can deal with it. She did."

One Bad Decision Away

This same father also told me that he tried to limit his involvement in his daughter's affairs to a one-sentence speech that he gave her as he was leaving campus after helping her get settled: "You're one bad decision away from ruining your life." He observed, "Guilt trip? Maybe. But my hope is that it would encourage her to think logically. So far, she's doing just that."

College Laundry: True Story

Sometimes opportunities for letting go or stepping aside present themselves in the most mundane of circumstances. The mother of a Notre Dame graduate told me this story about her son's experience with . . . laundry:

My son called me: "Is it OK if I sign up for the college laundry service? It only costs a bit more than doing it myself, but it saves a lot of time that I will be able to put to better use by studying."

I replied, "Fine by me."

Then, a couple of weeks later, my son called me again: "You won't believe this! But they lost my laundry! I dropped it off just the way I'm supposed to and now they've gone ahead and lost it! Incredible!"

I replied, "Maybe you should call the service." (Ain't no way *I* was going to call!)

So, my son went to the manager of the service who then produced a slip showing the date that the service had indeed received the items in question as well as the date that all the items, now cleaned and/or dry-cleaned, were returned to his dormitory.

A few days passed. Then came a call home. Her son sheepishly announced, "Problem solved. I found the clothes—[Pause]—on my roommate's bed. My bad."

The mother exclaimed to me, "Those clothes had to have been on that bed for a month and a half! Incredible!"

Needless to say, this mother had correctly decided that her son's laundry was not her issue.

When He/She Flunks Out: A Mother's Story

The mother of three college graduates told me about her response to what any parent would regard as a source of deep dread: *Her son flunked out of college.* What do you do when your kid is sent home from college?

Convinced beyond a doubt that her son's fate was sealed by his own actions of too little studying and too much partying, she and her husband were prepared to play a bit of hardball. The mother writes:

> So, how do you handle it when your immature adult child (who made some stupid mistakes) is asked to leave school? One of my sons (let's call him Brian) was caught engaging in activities that went against school policy and was asked to leave the school for

the rest of the semester. Of course, my husband, Sam, and I were devastated, as was Brian.

"Let's bring him home," was our first reaction. Then I started to think about it. Would rescuing Brian by letting him come home really help him? He was a twenty-one-year-old young man who needed to take hold of his life and stop making stupid choices. How would bringing him home help Brian learn that lesson? My husband and I went head-to-head on this.

Ironically, as a family counselor, I had written on this very subject and knew that we needed to get on the same page—but this was tough. I felt that Brian needed to take hold of his predicament and we, his parents, needed to let go of it. My heart broke but I could see he needed to feel the total effect of his failure and not be rescued by us. My husband was not so sure.

Believe it or not, my husband picked up the book *The Biggest Job We'll Ever Have* and re-read about Priorities No. 5 ("Value Success & Failure"), No. 6 ("Allow Obstacles to Become Opportunities"), and No. 7 ("Take Hold and Let Go"). Sam came to me tearfully that next day and said "You are right. He has to figure out something else to do. We cannot rescue him."

We called Brian and told him that he needed to find somewhere else to live. Despite his circumstances, some luck came his way when he called his uncle in Louisiana who was willing to let him come live with him for a time . . . if he paid rent and had a job. Brian moved there and worked at a restaurant.

His uncle treated him as an adult. He was expected to help take care of the yard, the house, to take his turn cooking—and pay rent. Working at Ruby Tuesday's, he learned to be a good waiter—and he also learned that he did not much like being a waiter! (In fact, he called one night to tell us that he thought it sucked . . . which his Dad and I thought was great. We also thought, "Hmmm, maybe this approach is working!") After a while, Brian came to believe that studying beat waiting on tables.

Brian called his school towards the end of the semester, re-interviewed to be readmitted, and convinced them to give him another shot. He went back to college and graduated two years later. Today, he has a great job and lives across the country. He is fiercely independent and is grateful for his education. He is a responsible worker who has earned accolades at his company. I'm proud to say that the Brian of today is praised for his integrity and his work ethic.

I sometimes wonder, had we not had the courage to require him to feel the full consequences of his actions, where would he be today? Where would we, his parents, be? I'm grateful I was able to "take hold" of my belief in him—the belief and confidence in his ability to figure out a solution to his problem—and "let go" of the outcome.

When the College Falls Short

Another mother of three graduates found herself able to let go of her children's behavior but found it hard to suppress her own dissatisfaction with what she perceived to be some of the school's shortcomings.

For example, she bristled at the fact that the college, claiming over-enrollment, had forced her daughter to live in a triple that was clearly meant for only two students. (The reality of the school's very high tuition price tag made this rooming accommodation all that much harder to take.) "However," she said, "I didn't call."

In another incident, when a daughter flunked a course, this same mother resisted the urge to call when she felt that the professor had been unfair. "Fair or unfair, it was something my daughter needed to work out on her own."

Rather than judge whether or not this parent had over- or understepped her bounds, the point is that she was clearly giving consideration to the role that was hers and was not hers to play in each situation. That's the point of Rule No. 4.

Roommate Issues—Six Stories

Roommate #1

The father of a James Madison University student told me about the time that his daughter called home during her freshman year complaining about her roommate. She stated that the two of them had nothing in common and said she was convinced that her roommate would agree with that. They even had differences regarding religion where the roommate was, in her opinion, overly vocal in proselytizing about her chosen faith.

She called her parents hinting that perhaps they could call the school and try to make other arrangements. However, her mother and father told her, "You need to work this out. It's only a year, and anyone should be able to put up with anyone for a year. When your sophomore year rolls around, you will be able to pick your roommate. So I'm afraid you're just going to have to suck it up and make the best of it."

The parents did not call the university, and the father told me that his daughter never really complained about it again. She got through the year, and while the two roommates never became the best of friends, they discovered and forged a relationship that worked for both of them, and the following year they both went off with their own friends. By the parents not acting, and not accepting responsibility for their daughter's issue, the daughter learned a valuable lesson about how to work out differences with others, and the parents permitted this lesson to occur as a result of their inaction.

Roommate #2

The mother of four college students told me that her involvement in her children's issues diminished as each child headed off to college. When she dropped off her first child at St. Michael's College (Vermont), she immediately sensed that her daughter and her roommate were not well matched. Not only did they seem to have nothing in common, they seemed to be sarcastically sniping at each other only a few hours after moving in to their room. The mother said,

I had a lump in my stomach as we drove away from campus. I
didn't think I should be feeling this way after writing such a
large tuition check! During my first few phone calls with my
daughter she talked incessantly of how much she disliked her
roommate.

Unable to take it any longer, I finally called the dean, who
responded, "Well, we have not received a formal complaint from
your daughter and we never act—if we act at all—until that
happens."

My daughter did ultimately contact the dean, and when she
did, she learned that I had beaten her to the punch. She was
furious with me for intervening, and for doing so behind her
back. She was right. It wasn't my issue. My daughter worked it
out. (They always do!) I learned to stay out of things.

Roommate #3

A story about my own roommate experience forty-plus years ago
may fit here. On a sunny September day in 1972 I first laid eyes on
my two college roommates. One was the first peer I had ever encountered who smoked a pipe (tobacco). He declined my offer to go
out and party that first night in favor of studying the course cata-
logue. While my spirits lifted upon discovering that the other guy
shared my love of the Rolling Stones, I quickly saw that he was a
more serious student than I could even pretend to be. The next day I
visited the dean and inquired about moving in with another guy I
knew down the hall. (For all I know, my two new roomies did
likewise.) The dean informed me that first-year room decisions were
final and essentially told me to "suck it up." I steeled myself for a
semester of "Dullsville."

Then, one September Saturday night, I entered a lively fraternity
house party to find a pack of seemingly cool folks singing around a
piano and engaged in compelling revelry. Working my way to the
center of the group, I was shocked to discover that the awesome
pianist at the bench was none other than my scholarly pipe-smoking
roommate. That night he owned that room. As I recall, the Stones
guy was there too. It was Dullsville no more. By Thanksgiving, the

three of us had become friends for life. Nearly four decades later, we still talk regularly.

I would never have dreamed of asking my parents for help or even advice on this matter—and I know what they would have said (i.e., "Suck it up!")—but I also didn't have a cell phone where I could spontaneously vent every emotion as it surfaced. Circumstances demanded that I sit with it and work it out. Today I'm glad I did.

Roommate #4

In "Don't Send in the Clones," Maureen Dowd writes of her own college roommate experiences: "I was dubious when I read in *The Wall Street Journal* last week that students are relying more on online roommate matching services to avoid getting paired with strangers or peers with different political views, study habits and messiness quotients."

Dowd continues, "The serendipity of ending up with roommates that you like, despite your differences, or can't stand, despite your similarities, or grow to like, despite your reservations, is an experience that toughens you up and broadens you out for the rest of life."

While acknowledging that she might well have used such sites had they been available during her undergraduate days, Dowd also points out that "co-habiting with snarly and moody roomies prepared me for the working world, where people can be outlandishly cantankerous over small stuff."

Dowd serves up some humorous anecdotes of her own college experiences. (I especially liked the one about the fight she had with a roommate who responded by leaving her stranded after dark in a "blighted" Washington, D.C. neighborhood, thereby teaching her an important lesson: *Never pick a fight with the driver.*) Then she presents her main point: "Choosing roommates who are mirror images may fit with our narcissistic and micro-targeted society, but it retards creativity and social growth." She believes that too many campuses are characterized by a "reluctance to mix it up" in those heated political and cultural debates so critical to campus life. As a result, many of our colleges and universities do seem eerily silent on social issues, as though fueled by a vibe of PC-harmony. [1]

Roommate #5

The mother of a Providence College student told me the story about her daughter coming home complaining about the fact that her roommate was eating all the food in their apartment. The roommate was neither contributing her fair share to pay for the food nor was she sharing in the cooking, and both these factors had contributed to a sense of resentment in her daughter.

One day the daughter called home and said, "Would you prepare some food for me that I can take back to school?"

Mom recalls:

> Before I could think about it, my first reaction was "sure I can do that," but my second thought was: I'm simply doing that in order to grab somewhat desperately for my daughter's love.
>
> The fact is, I don't really want to spend my time preparing this food, and I don't think it is the best thing for her. So, I turned to my daughter and said, "You know, you're probably going to want to be able to do some cooking in your adult life so maybe you should work on that now. At the same time, you might tell your roommate to stop being so stingy and demand that she contribute her fair share to the dining in your apartment."
>
> As it turned out, my daughter was fine with that. It took only a few seconds and the problem was solved. As my daughter prepares to leave college, I do sometimes find myself thinking I wish I had this mantra at the beginning of her career, but I'm not sure I would have listened to it then. We are all in a pretty good place now in terms of the dividing line separating our respective responsibilities.

Later in our interview, this same mother told me,

> This mantra makes a lot of sense. It took me a long time to realize that I was spending so much time on my children's issues

as a substitute for addressing personal issues in my own life. Specifically, I wasn't happy with my own profession, and rather than deal with that, I poured everything into my children. It wasn't good for them, and it wasn't good for me. I still sometimes catch myself making excuses for my kids' needs, but I also have taken great strides in simply not jumping in to address their issues.

Roommate #6

The mother of a University of Colorado student told me, "One time my daughter called me and said, 'My roommate is a pig. I can't live like this anymore! Something needs to be done!' I told her that she should go to the resident advisor. She responded, 'I already did. And nothing happened.' Hearing this, I went ahead and called the dean and tried to shake things up."

"However," she went on to say, "I would not do that today. My daughter needs to work out interpersonal relations with her peers and that's just not something I'm going to be able to help her with down the road. I wish I had not gotten involved. As I think about it, I can't even remember how it turned out!"

Disciplinary Trouble at School

The parent of a student at a New England private college told me about her struggles to step aside. Early in her daughter's time at college she tended to involve herself too often in roommate or course selection issues. Her daughter resented this and she backed off as a result. Then during her senior year, campus police arrested her daughter for public drunkenness. Mom said, "By then I was in a different place as a parent. My message to my daughter was frank and simple: 'I love you, but you've got to figure this out on your own.'"

Ironically, in the early years, this mother tended to intervene when her daughter didn't want her to. Now she found herself stepping aside despite her daughter's urgent requests for her to intervene and "fix" things.

Wanting to Call the College

The mother of three college graduates told me she almost called one school because "the college seemed to continually change the major requirements." She continues:

> One time my daughter even went so far as to receive a number of medical immunity shots to go on a field trip, and the field trip wound up being cancelled. Right or wrong, I chose not to call even though I remained unimpressed with the way the college handled this. In the end, my daughter graduated and has gone on with her life, and I didn't get bogged down with something that they probably weren't going to change anyway.

This same mother told me that there were two times when her children were in college that she wanted to call the administration to complain about something. The first was the incident when her daughter had been placed in a triple room that should have been a double (the second follows in the next section). The mother surmised that the school had over-enrolled—presumably more admitted students had chosen the school than had been predicted—and the dorms were over-crowded as a result. The mother wanted to call either to request a change or to request a decrease in the tuition she was paying. However, her daughter adamantly insisted that she not call; she honored her daughter's wishes, and as usually happens, her daughter worked the situation out and had a productive year in the school.

It is my sense that the overwhelming majority of today's parents would have serious difficulty trying to follow the example set by this mother and would have, thus, precluded the valuable learning experience the daughter received as a result of her mother stepping aside.

Wanting to Call . . . Even More!

Allow me to raise the pain threshold even more by describing the second case where this mother wanted to call, but again resisted the urge. Her daughter found herself in an academic disciplinary circumstance where her professor had charged her with failure to properly cite a source in a research paper. The professor decided that the matter was serious enough to require the student to drop the course. The daughter went to the dean, and the dean sided with her, believing that the daughter's failure to cite the source was an unfortunate but honest mistake and was in no way reflective of dishonest intent. The dean said this to the daughter and wrote the same point to the parents. At no time did the mother call anyone at the school. She commiserated with her daughter but also trusted her ability to handle and rise above the situation, and work matters out with the professor and the dean, which she did. Again, I doubt many parents today would act as this mother did.

At one point during my interview, I asked this mother if there had ever been a time when she did, in fact, call, and she described an interesting example. Her older daughter, also attending a prestigious liberal arts college, had remarked that very few students spoke up in class. She felt that too many of her classmates were sitting silently in a docile state listening to the words uttered by the professor and parroting them back to him in term papers and on exam essays. When the mother attended Parent's Weekend, she indeed observed very few students raising their hands to speak in the classes she attended. She was troubled by the fact that very few seemed to go out on a limb in stating their opinions or in challenging the professors in ways that students in the 1960s or 1970s might have.

Returning home after the weekend, she decided to raise this concern in a letter to the college president. She challenged him to look into this, suggesting that the school might either want to seek bolder, more courageous students during the admissions process . . . *or* . . . consider consciously challenging the students to speak up more in the classes. The mother was not sure if this violated the mantra of "Is this my issue?" or not, but it's interesting that her decision to contact the university had nothing to do with a motivation to extricate her daughter from a problem. It was solely to voice a concern about the school that was only tangentially related to her daughter.

When It *Is* Your Issue

When I spoke to the mother of three college children about this mantra, she said, "Our society guilts parents into believing that they need to jump in to solve their children's problems, that somehow they are being a neglectful parent if they don't fully immerse themselves in each and every one of their children's struggles."

She went on to say, "Anyone who is trying to be a good parent has heard that line, 'You are only as happy as your least happy child.' That is so wrong; so much bunk! Parents would do well to give the 'Is this my issue?' mantra a lot of careful consideration. I certainly wish I had considered it when my kids started in college."

Certainly there are occasions when it *is* the parent's issue. The mother of an NYU student told me, "I remembered a time when my son called me and said he needed to sign up for his classes and was denied by the registrar because his tuition hadn't yet been paid. They were not letting him sign up for his classes until the bill was paid. My son's father and I had made it clear to our children that we would pay the tuition bill so that indeed was my issue, and I needed to take care of that."

You and Your Spouse Don't Have to Agree

The parents of three college students told me of the jam that their middle daughter had gotten into. A guy at the college had asked her for a ride to the airport at the start of a vacation and she agreed. When the guy failed to show at the appointed hour, she went looking for him, eventually finding him asleep in his dorm room. She woke him up, helped him gather his things, and hurried him down to the car. She needed gas and her passenger offered neither financial contribution nor the effort to pump it. Running late, the daughter drove as fast as she could, managing to get her "friend" to the airport without a minute to spare. The guy hopped out of the car and never even thanked his driver. The daughter then fast-tracked back to the college to get her own things packed in order to make her own flight, now an iffy prospect thanks to the guy's tardiness.

The more she thought about this guy's rudeness and lack of appreciation, the more it bothered her. She ultimately called her parents, starting off the conversation with, "I'm such a sucker!" After thinking on it, the parents called the guy's father, whom they knew. The father responded with, "What do you want *me* to do about it? Why are you bothering me?" After that conversation, they were both angered and troubled by the father's callous disregard for his son's extreme rudeness toward their daughter. (As they say, "The apple doesn't fall far from the tree.")

When I asked the parents to evaluate their own actions regarding this incident, I got two opposing reactions.

Mom said, "I wish we had never gotten involved. Our daughter got the message: It's possible to be *too* kind. Don't let people take advantage of you. But we wasted our time with the father."

Dad disagreed, "I don't know. It's true that our daughter learned something and you're right, we got nowhere with the father, but parents need to be told when their kids act so inappropriately. Had our circumstances been in reverse, I'd want someone to tell me if my daughter had acted so selfishly."

A Daughter Advocates For and Receives a Merit Scholarship

The mother of a Dickinson College graduate told the story about how resisting the urge to interfere with her daughter's trials and tribulations not only caused her daughter to become more assertive, it may have even resulted in financial benefit. When her older daughter transferred from one liberal arts college to Dickinson, she was told that her new school would offer no merit scholarships for transfer students. This was troubling to her as money was tight in the family, and she had excelled at her previous school both academically and as an athlete.

In short, the daughter did not take "no" for an answer. She repeatedly approached the financial aid office and made her case, going so far as to state her belief that the college's position was unfair. While she will never know whether it was due to her high performance or to her badgering, she received a $10,000 merit scholarship her senior year. Her mother observed, "Not only did my daughter learn that persistence can pay off, I am absolutely convinced that had I or my husband tried to advocate for her, they would have easily dismissed us, and my daughter would have received no money. And as a bonus, to this day, when my daughter looks back on her college days, receiving that scholarship stands out as one of her proudest moments."

Professor Problems

The mother of an Elon University (North Carolina) student told me about the time her son called one night, very bummed out about a grade he had received on a paper. Exasperated, he said, "Professor Kingsfield (Not his real name, but one that fits . . . think, *Paper Chase*, the film) doesn't like the way I write."

The more their son talked, the more convinced both parents became that the problem had as much to do with clashing personalities as with writing style.

The mother said, "While we offered words of encouragement, we resisted the urge to intervene, even after Brian flunked the course. We told him, 'Brian, sometimes people don't like you and you've just got to learn to work something out with them.'"

The mother continues: "We knew that our son had an authority problem and we actually came to value this situation as meaningful preparation for our son's future life in the working world. Hey, the last thing you want to do with a kid with an authority problem is to rescue him from his interactions with authority figures."

In the end, their son graduated from Elon with a solid GPA. He indeed worked things out with his professors, and he did it on his own.

A Mother Asks for Help

The mother of four college graduates told me that her second son had performed reasonably well in the classroom and on the soccer field, but became filled with anxiety during the second semester of his senior year when his job prospects appeared dim. The closer graduation appeared, the more discouraged he became. Matters reached a point where he lost his voice—some kind of acute mega-laryngitis—and didn't even want to leave his dorm room. Very concerned, Mom called the soccer coach and asked if he would be willing to check in on her son.

The coach did as asked, and had a major positive impact. Ironically, the son had not reached out to his coach because he felt that their relationship was not very strong. In fact, he wasn't even sure if the coach liked him. In the end, not only did her son's disposition improve, the mother's intervention resulted in a new lifelong adult relationship for her son. The mother said, "Coach did what neither I nor my son's father could do. My son knew that his parents would always reach out to him, but his coach's actions taught him an important lesson about the inherent goodness in people and the fact that people aren't always what they seem."

Her son indeed graduated, worked a few years in the business world, and is currently enrolled in a prestigious MBA program.

Again, this mantra does not mean that parents should never get involved in their children's setbacks, only that they should give some thought to letting their children handle their own challenges, or, as in this case, sometimes ask someone else for help.

If there Is an Issue . . . Who Owns It?

Another priority in *The Biggest Job We'll Ever Have*, Priority No. 7, is called "Take Hold & Let Go." When we sent our kids off to college, my wife Laura and I often found it very important to give serious thought to this dynamic. During the parent workshops she and I facilitate, Laura frequently observes, "It seems that for most parents, the taking hold part comes a bit easier than the letting go part. Therefore, as moms and dads, we do well to give some serious thought ahead of time to what the issues are that are going to fit in the Take Hold compartment and which ones in the Letting Go one. It's pretty hard to make those decisions in real time on the fly."

Letting go may well be the prominent theme for parents of teenagers. Laura, the actual originator of the "Is this my issue?" mantra, observes:

> When your children are struggling, remember that it is *their* issue, not yours. For example, let's say you are convinced your child has an unhealthy relationship with alcohol or drugs while they are in college. Be sure to remind yourself that your child has an issue with drugs or alcohol, but you do not (unless, of course, you happen to have an issue of your own with substance abuse). So, you might well recommend that your son or daughter get some help, either with a counselor or a Twelve-Step group or any number of sources of help. And you should consider something like Al-Anon or some way to get help for someone who loves someone with substance abuse problems, but don't take that issue on as your own.

The Value of Doing It Wrong

I interviewed the mother of three college graduates who said, "You know, the 'Is this my issue?' mantra is a really good one. But I'd go a step further. If your kid comes to you for the solution to a problem, and you're on the fence (relative to this mantra) . . . I'd say, go with 'No.'"

When I pressed her to explain, she answered, "It's so much more of a greater and more meaningful learning process if they figure it out themselves, even if they do it wrong."

This same mother went on to tell me a story of her oldest son's college application process.

> In the early going, he announced to his father and me that he wasn't planning to visit any of the colleges he was applying to. He figured he would visit after he was admitted. My husband and I didn't exactly think that this was a very prudent way to proceed, but we said nothing. It turned out that he didn't get admitted into the schools he was most interested in attending. It also dawned on him that he had probably hurt his chances by not interviewing. Then he shifted into high gear and took control of his responsibility with a heightened sense of initiative. In the end, he wound up at the University of Colorado, a school he loved, and from which he graduated. He also learned some valuable lessons on how to best plan and prepare for his future.

Life Is an "And" . . . Not an "Or"

Another quote that my wife originated for our parent workshops is appropriate here: "Life is an 'and' not an 'or.'" Let's say you believe that your child is partying too much. You might say, "Honey, I'm proud of the academic work you're doing . . . and I also think you should consider taking a look at your drinking habits." Although a subtle difference, this approach is softer in tone than "Yeah, you're doing pretty well in school, but you're drinking too much."

The simple choice of *and* instead of *but* or *or* allows for a dispassionate observation that is not as loaded with innuendo. It also allows the speaker to be true to him- or herself by not holding on to resentments, and it perhaps provides an environment more conducive to the receiver giving serious thought to the point being made.

NOTE

1. Maureen Dowd. "Don't Send in the Clones," *New York Times*, August 11, 2010.

Rule No. 5

GET CURIOUS

The greatest burden a child must bear is the unlived life of the parents. —Carl Jung

Children are educated by what the grownup is and not by what he says. — Carl Jung

Next year, our fourth child will enter college and now we've got so much time on our hands, especially since we realized that how they do in college is their business, their problem. We didn't know that the first couple times around. —Mother of four college students

My Take:

- Of Novels and Harmonicas

Parent Anecdotes and Stories:

- Moving to Maine
- Teaching in an Urban Charter School
- Fun and Mind-Expanding Trips
- Too Unselfish
- Same Company, New Job

- Home . . . Not a Homestead
- Back to Reading
- From Stockbroker . . . to Mom . . . to Social Worker
- From Teaching to Parenting and Back (to Teaching)
- From Lawyer . . . to Mom . . . to Child Psychology
- Community Service and Gardening
- eBay Business
- From Hobby to Second Career
- If I Had It to Do Over . . .
- "Do the Right Thing"
- Need for Rigor and Follow-through
- Words from Lifelong Learners: My Colleagues

MY TAKE

Go to any college website and you will invariably find a mission statement that involves the goal of graduating lifelong learners. When you think about it, isn't that the point? Don't get me wrong, I certainly hope my children and yours will ultimately pass their exams and acquire the necessary credits in order to graduate with a respected degree. However, I would be saddened if their enterprising curiosity concluded upon receipt of their diploma.

Of Novels and Harmonicas

The essence of Rule No. 5 is a simple claim: If you want your child to be a life-long learner, you might do well to commit to being one yourself. In my case, shortly after my first child headed off to college, I picked up the harmonica. I had long been fascinated by the instrument and especially by the great blues men. I had even picked it up a few times before, only to put it back down in fairly short order. This time I stayed with it until I was able to pass for competent in some blues jam sessions whereupon I was forever hooked. I'll never forget that feeling when a stranger came up to me and said, "Yo, you blow a mean harp, man." (Hey, I doubt he realized that my repertoire was limited to a simple alternation between two notes, and two notes only, but the compliment still felt great!) This new avocation, in turn, led me to another as an amateur collector of books on jazz and popular music.

I don't know how impressed my children are by the fact that their old man has picked up the harmonica, and I certainly didn't start playing it to impress them, but I see it as a good thing for all concerned. Looking back, I recall that my father picked up golf in his mid-forties, right around the time I was heading to college. He committed himself to excelling at it, becoming a student of the game, practicing and playing pretty much every day. He wound up shooting his age several times in his seventies and eighties, an accomplishment never achieved by many lifelong golfers, even good ones. While I can't say that I was consciously inspired by his efforts in golf, I definitely believe that it had a positive effect on my subconscious.

A second way that I got curious involved a fairly simple task: reading. My work requires me to travel often, and for years I would generally read non-fiction books while waiting in airports, while airborne, or in hotel rooms. I suppose this made me feel as though I was still engaged in work and setting an example while traveling. (Some coworkers perceive travel as glamorous and carefree, but most who do a lot of it will agree that it gets old fast!) I would then try to return to campus with a few tidbits of wisdom that I picked up in a book about business management, teaching, or psychology.

Around the time my second daughter headed off to college, I switched my reading over to fiction and found myself getting lost in novels. Upon returning home or to campus I would converse with colleagues or try to get my wife and daughters turned on to the latest book I had read. They (specifically, my daughters) would often respond by teasing me or scoffing at "Dad's latest kick." I would take my medicine from them good-naturedly, all the while remembering the effect that my dad's pursuit of golf had had on me.

It could well be that I'm deluding myself in believing that either my harmonica playing or novel reading are having any effect on my daughters, to say nothing of whether that effect is subconscious or of any other kind. However, even if it is having no effect, both are definitely enriching the quality of *my* life. And the whole point of "get curious" is its potential to be mutually beneficial to our children and to us as parents, as people.

While I don't believe he had children, I repeat the quote attributed to James Baldwin (1924–1987), one I have used many times when working with families: "Children have never been very good at listening to their elders, but they never fail to imitate them."

You can probably guess where I am going with this. If you commit to being a life-long learner, you will be sending a powerful message to your child even if he/she jokes about it or scoffs at you. And, as was the case with my father's golf, it can be a powerful message even if they don't realize it at the time. As Baldwin's quote suggests, they are paying attention all the time. Not only can your actions speak louder than words, they can also leave a powerful legacy.

This view is supported in two quotes attributed to Swiss psychiatrist Carl Jung (1875–1961). The first has long been the subject of debate among educators and family counselors: "The greatest burden a child must bear is the unlived life of the parents." (Another version of the quote: "Nothing has a stronger influence psychologically on their environment and especially on their children than the unlived life of the parent.")

Suffice it to say that Jung's quote goes well beyond Baldwin's message that actions speak louder than words. In fact, Jung seemed to be saying that *in*action speaks louder than both of them!

My sisters and I knew that our parents loved us and made raising us their highest priority, but we also knew that they pursued deep interests that had nothing to do with us. These interests went far beyond those of basic recreation. Our mother voluntarily taught ballet to elementary school children, volunteered at our local hospital, and wrote an awful lot of poetry.

For more than half a century our father has dedicated his life to a B.H.A.G.—Big, Hairy, Audacious Goal. (This term is presented and explained in the book *Built to Last: Successful Habits of Visionary*

Companies by James Collins and Jerry Porras [New York: Harper Business Solutions, 1994].) He has never wavered from nor shied away from his lifelong commitment to find a better way to educate all American kids. Through successes and failures, he keeps his eye on the prize. Our parents often told us that no job was more important to them than "raising our kids to be better people than we are." However, they also showed us that they had lives of their own— both at work and at play.

The second quote by Jung echoes Baldwin's message: "Children are educated by what the grownup is and not by what he says." During my career as an educator, I have facilitated more parent-teacher conferences than I could count. While people may be willing to talk about their problems more now than they were when I began in the 1970s, one dysfunctional scenario continues to present itself over and over again: a parent talking on-and-on ad infinitum to a teenager who is totally zoned out:

> The *parent* is thinking: *If I can just string together the right combination of words, then the light will go on in my kid's head and all will be right in the world.*
> *I'm* thinking: *1) You can't; 2) It won't.*
> The *kid* is thinking one thing, and one thing only: *Whatever* .

Baldwin and Jung remind us to be ever mindful in how we prioritize what we say, what we do, and who we are. I like to say, "Never kid a kid." They will always know what is really important to us. Not only are they watching what we do, Jung tells us that they are also internalizing what we do *not* do. The best thing we can do is live our own lives to the fullest. Here are some anecdotes and stories from parents striving to do just that.

PARENT ANECDOTES AND STORIES

Moving to Maine

The mother of three college graduates proudly told me,

> My husband and I completely reinvented ourselves after our
> children went off to college. First, we moved from the busy D.C.
> suburbs of Virginia to the quiet (and beautiful!) coast of Maine.
> Then, after twenty-three years as a homemaker, I went to work
> full time and began a career working with families. For his part,
> my husband walked away from a successful corporate life to do
> something entrepreneurial with his own start-up company.

Teaching in an Urban Charter School

Another mother of three graduates said,

> As soon as we got our kids off to college, we did two things that
> we always wanted to do. First, after having spent thirty years
> teaching in a New England boarding school, we took a two-year
> sabbatical working in an urban charter school. Those two years
> amounted to one of the most rewarding experiences of our ca-
> reer. We also like to think that they also set an example for our
> children.

"The second thing we did," she said,

> was plan some travel trips that we have always wanted to take.
> As a result, we have since been to New Zealand, Scotland, and
> Africa. (We did take the kids to Africa where our oldest had
> founded a nonprofit organization that seeks to give micro-loans
> to small businesses and enterprising individuals in western Afri-
> ca.)

The mother continued,

Come to think of it, we also experienced a third benefit after we got our kids through college. We pooled our newfound "wealth"—that is, the money we had been spending on college tuition was now ours!—and then applied it to renovating the lakeside cottage that had been an integral part of our family for so many years and will now continue to be well into the future.

Fun and Mind-Expanding Trips

One of my own college friends who has sent three kids to college told me,

> My wife and I are convinced that the best way to enrich our kids' lives is to travel to places that open their eyes. We have taken them away from the traditional tourist locations—no weeks in Nantucket or Kiawah for us. We have chosen to visit Istanbul, Morocco, Mexico, Prague, and Costa Rica over the past few years. These visits are fun and mind expanding.

Too Unselfish

The mother of a University of Maine graduate said,

> I've always put my kids first. You know, you can almost be too unselfish. I've got one more kid to get through school, but I don't plan to wait to get my master's. I have always had a dream to do something in the arena of counseling women to be better people. There's no need to wait to get started on this. My kid can get through college on his own!

Same Company, New Job

The mother of four college students told me that she made a transition at work, staying with the same company but moving from human relations to technology. "This enabled me to keep working with people I love while transitioning to a new learning curve with new and different responsibilities," she said.

This woman's husband told me that he had discovered the joys of books on tape which, in turn, has led to a newfound interest in "learning all that stuff that I might have learned in high school had I been paying attention."

Mom said, "Next year, our fourth child will enter college and now we've got so much time on our hands, especially since we realized that how they do in college is their business, their problem. We didn't know that the first couple times around."

Mom's comment brings to mind the old adage about an irony of life: It must be lived forward but can only be understood in reverse.

The mother of three college students told me a similar message. "Once my kids went off to college," she said, "my career took off! I attended conferences and got new training to become current with all the latest thinking in my profession. I got a new lease on life at work."

Another mother, one with two children in college, decided to transition from the department of sales to that of marketing in the business she and her husband established when their children were young. She said, "I took a course in marketing at Northwestern University, learned a lot of fascinating new information, and emerged re-energized to take on a new role in our company."

Home . . . Not a Homestead

One mother told me a story about her own experiences after graduating from college. She had done very well as a college student and was home visiting while looking for a job, when her father calmly, but firmly announced, "This is a home, not a homestead. You are now a college graduate with a head start in the world that most people your age would envy. Therefore, you no longer live in this home. You are a guest, and you are welcome to stay for periods of up to two weeks. Anything longer than that, we will need to work out some kind of rent arrangement."

When she first heard this, she thought that her father was being overly harsh. Then she found herself saying essentially the same thing to her own children when they returned from college. While some might consider this cold, I can tell you that this family is among the closest that I know.

Back to Reading

The father of a Sacred Heart University student told me that being an empty nester didn't lead him to take on a whole host of new hobbies, but it did free him up to reconnect with some of his passions, namely reading. As he told me, "It's been absolutely great to get back to my old practice of reading one or two books per week. In fact, it feels like a luxury."

From Stockbroker . . . to Mom . . . to Social Worker

The mother of two college graduates told me that before she had children she had spent ten productive years as a New York City stockbroker. Then when the children came along, she stepped away from work and focused all of her time on raising her children. When the first one went off to college and she was able to catch her breath, she realized that she missed the challenges of being in the work force, but she also didn't think she wanted to return to the financial services industry. She had always been intrigued by the idea of social work, and at the suggestion of a friend, she decided to audit a course in the subject at Fordham University. She was surprised by the interest sparked by this course: "While it was not the most interesting class, it was the first time I was engaged in the process of academic learning as a 'full-fledged' adult (forty-four years old). I never thought I would want to go back to school, but I really loved it."

Needless to say, her interest did not end when this course concluded. She said,

> One of the brightest moments for me with my family and my "getting curious" is when my husband, daughter, and son sat in the audience as I graduated from the post graduate program at the Ackerman Institute for the Family (New York City). It was an intimate graduation, about fifteen of us, but it was very special. I started the program while my kids were both in college and finished it after they graduated. I saw the pride in their faces as they saw me accomplishing something personal. . . . That meant so much to me.

After earning her master's degree, this mother earned her license to practice and today is a family and couples therapist in New York City. In talking with her, it was clear that she is invigorated by her new career, and I would imagine that her children are inspired by her life choice. She has certainly been a great role model in this respect.

From Teaching to Parenting and Back (to Teaching)

The mother of four college graduates told me,

> After studying elementary education in college and teaching for five years, I gave it all up to be a stay-at-home mom for twenty-three years. After helping get the first three through college, I began to think seriously about returning to the classroom as my fourth entered high school. I was also intrigued about the high school level, thinking that it might be more intellectually stimulating. So, I made the necessary preparations and today I teach high school English and I love it!

From Lawyer . . . to Mom . . . to Child Psychology

Another mother told me of a similar progression in her life after her two kids went off to college. She said,

> I started out in my professional life as a lawyer. I liked it, but I had always been interested in kids and psychology. This interest

was furthered and tested (!) when I turned my total attention to raising two boys. Then when they headed off to college, I decided not to go back to law. Instead, I pursued and received a master's degree in child development and am gearing up to make a fulltime professional move in this direction. It's exciting!

Community Service and Gardening

The mother of three college students said, "Your adult children are never too old to appreciate healthy modeling from their parents." This particular parent got deeply involved in the homeless community in her town. She said, "I believe I made a positive contribution to the lives of the homeless in our city, and I know this work made me feel very good about myself. I also think it set an example for my children that I hope they will choose to follow."

The same mother excitedly told me about her new hobby of gardening. When her first crop of eggplant successfully came out on the vine, she sent photos of her crop to all of her kids. One of them replied, "Great job, Mom! I always wanted to do that. I look forward to coming home and having a salad with you." She said, "That might seem small, but it sure made me feel good."

eBay Business

The father of three college graduates writes:

> Once our children headed off to college (private college . . . big $$$), it became apparent that money was going to be tight. When our oldest began college, we went through several initial months of paying off the bills . . . which now included a hefty monthly payment plan for college . . . only to realize we had only a couple hundred discretionary dollars to get us through to the next pay period.
>
> Thus, necessity being the mother of invention, I launched my eBay business. With a basement full of items (both my wife and I are pack rats), I decided to earn a few extra dollars by selling

off our accumulation of goods that had been sitting around for
years. After some initial success, I found eBay becoming a hobby—a fun and productive one that brought new money in, instead of sending earned money out. The extra $200-$500 that
eBay would bring in monthly was enough to decrease the financial pressure of living from paycheck to paycheck. My wife even
got into the action by finding items at Goodwill and other thrift
stores that had value and ultimately netted a fine return for us on
eBay.

With our three children, we went through nine consecutive
years of private college tuitions. Not only did eBay help take the
financial sting out of this period in our lives, it was fun.

And let us remember, "fun" is a good thing.

From Hobby to Second Career

The mother of three college graduates told me that she had always
been interested in alternative and holistic medicine. She dabbled in
the study of the topic while her kids were growing up. Once her
three sons had all headed off to college and out of the house, she
realized, "You know, I could do this on another level." She then
turned this interest into a second career helping individuals who
want to explore the use of alternative and holistic medicine as a way
to pursue and maintain a healthy lifestyle.

If I Had It to Do Over . . .

The mother of two college graduates told me that, if she could do it
all over again, she wished she had just slowed down, stepped aside
in the very beginning and let her kids figure it all out. She had
reached this place of serenity by the time her second child was off at
college but had been very uptight when the first one went. She said,

There's this competition of what everyone else is doing that
feeds on both the kid and the parent. You can't help but try to

keep up with the Joneses either by surpassing whatever they're
doing or at least not doing anything as badly as others are doing
things. In the end, it's your kids' education; it's not yours. I think
I figured that out near the end of the experience, and I wish I had
gotten on that wavelength a bit earlier.

"Do the Right Thing"

The mother of three college graduates told me,

> Well, yeah, after our kids headed off to college, I dabbled in
> some hobbies . . . oil painting, for example. But, more than that,
> I'm just out there enjoying life. My husband and I retired from
> the successful business we founded, we contribute our time to a
> non-profit board, and we do a lot of travelling.

Her husband continued,

> Our family has long had a two-part motto. First, *Do the right
> thing.* Second, *You should know what that is.* And if you don't
> know, do whatever you need to do to find out. That's worked in
> our lives and we have tried to pass that along to our kids. It's a
> good philosophy before, during, and after college.

It's also good for college students, their parents, and anybody
else . . . at any time.

Need for Rigor and Follow-through

Hopefully, some of these stories have served to heighten your imag-
ination for some possibilities for yourself. As the mother of a Clark
University student observes, in stream-of-consciousness style, there
is no shortage of possibilities:

> Get curious. Hmm . . . I think I should take a yoga class. . . . I
> would really like to go to the wine-tastings sponsored by a local
> cooking store. . . . I've always wanted to go to the Boothbay

(Maine) Botanical Gardens. . . . Did you know that Friday nights are free at the Portland Museum of Art? . . . Do you know that admission is always free at the Bowdoin Art Museum? . . . I've heard that the C. G. Jung Center in nearby Brunswick offers fascinating lectures in analytical psychology. . . . I've always thought that I could teach a gluten-free cooking class.

My problem is not so much with curiosity as it is with rigor and follow-through. I could get curious about why that is."

Couldn't we all!

If this mother has this many opportunities in the rural environs of midcoast Maine, well, then you urban and suburban folks have no excuse not to throw yourselves into a whole lot of stuff! So, go on and Get Curious!

Words from Lifelong Learners: My Colleagues

At the Hyde Schools where I work, I am fortunate to be surrounded by a faculty of lifelong learners. One day it dawned on me: Why not ask my colleagues if they were, in fact, inspired by the activities of their own parents during and after their own college days? So, I went into a faculty meeting and did exactly that. Here are some of the responses I received.

A University of Connecticut graduate, also the mother of four college students, said, "When my siblings and I left the house, my mother decided to go back to college and get her bachelor's degree. She went from waitress/stay-at-home mom to full-time student. I remember thinking, 'If she can do this I certainly need to succeed in college as well!!'"

A Juniata College graduate, also the mother of two college graduates said,

> After I went to school, my mother went to work in my father's business—a family-owned furniture store. Until that time, the business had been small, focusing on appliances, mattresses, kitchen tables, etc. With mom's decorative flair, they expanded the inventory to include furniture for all rooms in the house and

she quadrupled the volume of business they did. . . . Speaking more personally, after my second graduated from college, I went back for my master's at Columbia.

Another colleague, a recent college graduate said, "When I went to Middlebury and my younger sister moved to Taipei for college, my dad began running almost every morning with a group of friends. He went on to complete two marathons. My mom joined a service group at church and took Japanese lessons once a week."

A University of Connecticut graduate remembers,

> As if my mother returning to school in her late thirties to pursue a dream to become a teacher wasn't enough inspiration, her mother (my grandmother) started college in her sixties to become a social worker. She completed her undergrad and MSW degrees and then began working with at-risk youth in New Haven. She kept that job until being let go this year at the age of ninety. My grandparents were comfortably retired at that time which proves she took on these inspiring challenges all for the love of true learning and teaching. In addition to inspiring my curiosity, it meant I could not quit on my journey. If my mother could do it while raising four kids and running a full time day care from the home, and my grandmother could do what she did in her sixties, seventies, and eighties, what excuse could I have to not go after change in myself?

A Massachusetts College of Liberal Arts graduate with a daughter headed to college wrote:

> I immediately thought back to all the driving my family did whether to hockey games or family trips. During the trips my father was fairly lenient to what we listened to as long as at the top and bottom of each hour he could get updated on the news. I remember being puzzled and wondering, "What could have possibly changed in thirty minutes?" Unfazed, my father insisted on this routine and rarely (think: never) did we try to change it back to music until he was satisfied with the news update.

When I was in high school, I discovered that I was among the more informed or even "enlightened" kids in my class. Most kids seemed oblivious to anything happening around the world, especially due to the rise of MTV at the time. During my freshman year of college, I realized that I had fallen into the habit of listening to the news. I remember walking into an economics class and the professor was asking about what had just happened in the Philippines. I was the only one among a class of twenty students who knew that Ferdinand Marcos had fled the country and that a new government had taken control.

From that point forward, I continued to listen to the news. It has become part of my daily routine and I hear my daughter (sometimes my wife, too) complaining about listening to the news. Then again, I hear from many of my daughter's teachers that she is highly knowledgeable about the world around her. In fact, she wrote her college essay on how she is different from her generation because she is not wrapped up in social media and pop culture.

My recommendation to those going off to college: Take a break from the music and listen to a news report twice an hour. It could pay off in ways that are not fully understood at the moment.

A recent Suffolk University graduate said,

> After I headed off to college my father began to compete heavily in triathlons and cycling competitions. His personal quest for physical fitness has not only been an inspiration to me, but has also made a notable difference in his overall demeanor.

As Bob Dylan sings, "He [who is] not busy being born is busy dying." As the above stories and anecdotes hopefully demonstrate, "getting curious" is good for all concerned. It sets a great example for our children and it is fun and exciting for us. So, let's get busy being born!

EPILOGUE

Something for Kids and Parents to Read Together

Playing the Odds: College Admissions

- My Experience (circa 1972)
- A Crap Shoot
- The Cult of Self-Esteem
- Get Your Confidence from Who You Are

When I am approached to speak to high school students and their parents about college readiness, I am reluctant to accept any engagements before May 1 of any given school year. This is because the college application process has become such a deeply engrossing, angst-producing gauntlet for high school seniors and their families that I simply prefer not to speak to them until the colleges have communicated their acceptances and/or rejections. I much prefer to talk to the kids and their parents *after* they know where they are headed in the fall.

At the same time, since so much of the senior year can be preoccupied with "The Decision," I thought I would conclude this book with a few thoughts on how kids and parents might consider the ordeal of the college application process. While my two books are designed for separate audiences, this conclusion is offered in the spirit of something that students and parents might read and discuss together as a family.

MY EXPERIENCE (CIRCA 1972)

When I applied to college forty years ago, I recall a fun and exciting time with minimal parental intervention. After visiting ten or so colleges, all on my own or with friends (i.e., neither of my parents came on any of my visits), I ultimately applied to four, all in the "Most Selective" category. My teenaged naiveté had me thinking that I would get into at least one of them and featured a hazy back-up plan involving a partially filled out application (stuffed somewhere in my bureau drawer) for a school with "rolling" admissions that I perceived, realistically or not, as a sure thing. If I ended up going 0 for 4—a far more likely outcome than my boundless naiveté could have processed at the time—I figured I'd either take a shot at the "rolling" option or simply take a year off.

Come April, I went 2 for 4. My "plan" worked. (Who says "dumb luck" isn't a legitimate strategy?)

Looking back on those days, I remember feeling like, well, an adult. I was doing adult things. My parents were certainly interested in my college plans, but when we talked about it over the dinner table—remember the dinner table?—I remember feeling like an adult conversing with fellow adults about my hopes and plans. To be sure, I still had plenty of capacity for juvenilia—a capacity I indeed took with me to college—but the process was a positive step in my coming of age.

If you are a parent or a high school teacher, I don't need to tell you that times have changed. For one thing, it is not unusual for today's high school seniors to apply to more than a dozen colleges. For another, many of them seem surrounded by adult "handlers," be they parents or professional counselors. For better or worse, these days the college application cycle can be stressful for both students and parents. So, for those embroiled in the admission process, here are a few words—some supportive, some maybe not—to consider.

A CRAP SHOOT

Any high school senior who applies to those schools listed in the "Most Selective" category would do well to accept the endeavor as a crap shoot. A quick look at the *U.S. News & World Report* selectivity rankings (or those of many similar college admissions oriented websites) shows that the fifty most selective colleges present a very poor set of odds ranging anywhere from a 6 percent to a 24 percent acceptance rate. Your prospects aren't all that much better with the next fifty: 24 percent to 33 percent.

Today's "We regret to inform you" letters basically riff on the same message I got in 1972: *Your credentials are indeed impressive, but. . . . We had many more qualified applicants than we could admit. . . . In fact, (insert college name)'s current popularity has resulted in yet another significant increase in our number of applicants. . . . Don't take it personally. . . . We wish you luck, etc.* (I swear, these admissions offices must attend the same conferences!)

These letters, while truthful, obscure the whole story.

Even if you manage to meet the qualifications of the *publicly* stated criteria (SAT, GPA, rank in class, etc.), you then get compared against a moving target in the form of annually changing secret criteria. To keep their anxiety in check, I tell high school seniors to assume that there are multiple *private* conversations going on behind closed doors at your dream school that might go like this:

- "Enough with these illiterate athletes!"
- "We need more oboe players."
- "Dial down the Northeast kids; let's give priority to Seattle kids."
- "It's high time we address alumni concerns about our enrollment's cultural diversity."

And on and on.

And to amplify the "on and on" factor, remember that each one of these criteria also has a mirror opposite:

- "We need *more* stud athletes!"
- "Enough with the oboe players."
- "Forget east/west, how do we get some southern kids in here?"

Well, you get the idea. . . .

To review thus far:

- Secret criteria exists.
- You are *not* in on the secret.

To compound confusion, also realize that the "Most Selectives" will welcome your application with a smile, regardless of how qualified . . . or *un*qualified . . . you may happen to be. After all, an oversupply of unqualified candidates enables them to maintain their *uber* selective status. All of the admissions websites—U.S. News, Huffington Post, College Prowler, Unigo, and the like—present their selectivity rankings based solely on absolute numbers: total applicants versus number admitted.

For example, the 1,600 lucky individuals who began in September 2013 as members of Harvard's Class of 2017 began their aspirations to attend Harvard as members of an applicant pool consisting of 35,023 high school seniors, 2,029 of whom were ultimately admitted (see The Harvard Gazette at www.harvard.edu). Not only are these odds—5.8 percent—worse than those presented by a Las Vegas casino, you must accept the fact that you will never get to know where you stood in the queue.

When you get right down to it, it's up to you to determine whether you have a real shot at receiving an acceptance letter or whether you're wasting your time. Hence, one simple step applicants and their parents can take is to seek some informed and objective counsel. (Don't limit yourselves to talking with each other!)

THE CULT OF SELF-ESTEEM

Some of my colleagues have accused me of unfairly trashing the colleges. Perhaps I should better explain my vantage point. After more than thirty-five years of trying to help hundreds of kids navigate the college admissions landscape, I believe we have arrived at an unhealthy juncture with the colleges, the secondary schools, the parents, and even the kids complicit in our current state of affairs. Since I spend my days working with kids, they remain the focus of my efforts.

A generation ago, back before the "Cult of Self-Esteem" took such a firm hold on our families and within our schools, college applicants pretty much owned the process and took the good with the bad. Parents were nowhere near as engaged as they are today. In those pre-*everybody-gets-a-trophy* days, most kids had already had experience with setbacks. In my case, I recall getting cut from a middle school hockey team. I also remember a middle school football season where the sum total of my playing time was a single kick-off in a losing cause. (Thankfully, those years were my athletic nadir. That is, if you don't count right now.) The football experience was especially hard to take, more than a bit humiliating, given the fact that my father had been a highly respected football coach. It never would have occurred to my parents to badger the coach to give me more playing time. It never would have occurred to me to ask them to do so. And this dynamic was also true of my peers and their parents.

Most of us had also experienced some triumphs. It's not that we didn't experience disappointment when we were rejected by our dream colleges. It's just that, as a rule, we were better equipped to handle rejection than today's kids, if for no other reason than the fact that we had more practice with it than today's kids have had.

If you think about it, a kid whose bedroom bureau is fully cluttered with trophies. Or who has never been cut from an athletic team. Or whose helicoptering mom or dad has been running interference for them since first grade, may not have had much chance to process success and failure. For many of these, the college admissions process is the first realization that life is *not* "sanitized for your protection."

I figure that if today's high school kids have a better understanding of the game going in, they'll be better able to handle the outcomes, be they good or bad.

GET YOUR CONFIDENCE FROM WHO YOU ARE

In the end, the colleges are addressing their realties as they feel they must. So must the applicants. As one who represents the applicants in the dynamic, it is my job to make sure they understand who is holding the cards. (That would be the colleges.) I have also found an increasing need to go overboard in helping them truly gain that understanding.

I long for a game-changing admissions department to actually say to an applicant, "As impressive a candidate as you are, I must tell you that you are unlikely to be admitted here. Would you like me to give you a few suggestions of schools that might be a better fit for you?" While I am hopeful that this will someday happen, the current structure of college rankings presents a disincentive to the admissions departments to act in this way. So, in the meantime, should a friendly poker-faced college admissions officer encourage you to apply to your dream school, by all means, go ahead. Just don't lose sight of the gambler's maxim: The odds always favor the house. Furthermore, you might do well to consider the probability that the owner of that poker face has a mandate from his or her superior to increase the number of applicants to that very school you may now covet.

To be fair, I have also encountered a number of colleges striving to be part of the solution. For example, not only am I a fan of the organization Colleges that Change Lives— check out their website at www.ctcl.org—we've had their representatives speak to our seniors where I work at Hyde Schools. I would also conclude that most of the college admissions officers I have encountered do indeed genuinely care about the applicants to their schools. (Just keep in mind that they also genuinely care about their own job performance reviews.)

One day, about twenty years ago, when I was wearing the headmaster hat at Hyde School, a young woman burst into my office to excitedly tell me that she had just been admitted to the school of her dreams, Colgate University. I was excited for her. I congratulated her as she had worked hard at our school, exhibiting commendable citizenship, athletic prowess, and academic scholarship during her years with us. We also shared a chuckle over the fact that about twenty years before, I had received a rejection letter from the very same school.

Then as we were concluding our conversation, I couldn't resist succumbing to a mischievous temptation I felt to tweak her. I caught her off guard with a rather direct question: "So, tell me, are you a better person than you were yesterday?"

She responded, "Huh? What do you mean?"

I pushed ahead, "Well, yesterday you didn't have this letter. Today you do. So, are you better person today because of it?"

She thought for a moment and responded, "Well, yeah, I guess so. . . . But then maybe not. . . . Uhm. . . . Oh, My God! . . . I don't know."

Intending to relieve the misery I had caused (and feeling a bit guilty about it), I said, "Hey, I'm very happy for you. You have worked hard and you definitely deserve the good things that are happening to you right now. However, my hope for you in your life is that you won't get your confidence from what others decide about you. . . . You'll get it from who you are. I'm genuinely delighted that your first choice school admitted you, but, let me ask you, how would you be feeling right now if that letter you are holding was very thin and started out with 'We regret to inform you' . . . ?"

She replied, "I'd be sad."

Me: "OK, but would you think less of yourself?"

She: "I'm not sure."

Me: "It may sound funny, but this school chose to let you into their club. Their decision says as much about them as it does about you. Your profile lined up with what they were looking for. If it makes you feel better, I would say that they have excellent taste. I want you to know that my opinion of you, an opinion of affection and respect, is unchanged by their decision. And as a teacher who cares about you, I'm trying to move you toward the same place."

When all is said and done, good luck, but remember, whatever they decide—up or down—says a little about you and a whole lot about them. Never let your self-confidence be determined according to others' assessment of your worthiness. That decision is yours . . . and yours alone.

So, now it's time to get down to business. During my research, I was fortunate to speak with Pat Bassett, a nationally respected educational consultant who recently completed a distinguished tenure as president of the National Association of Independent Schools. He told me about some advice that he frequently gives to high school seniors in commencement speeches:

> In class, especially in lecture classes, be the first to ask a question. You'll be noticed by the professor if you show interest by being engaged. He or she will learn your name. Show up for office hours. If you can develop a relationship with a professor, your college experience will be immensely deepened.

Great points. Wish I had learned them before *College Success Guaranteed* went to press!

ACKNOWLEDGMENTS

I am grateful for the assistance that so many offered to me in the course of preparing and writing this book.

First, I thank the scores of Hyde parents—past and present—who honestly and openly shared their personal stories, both the triumphs and the setbacks.

My Hyde colleagues were also extremely helpful, especially Cindy Warnick who provided her considerable editorial expertise.

Ann Peden, my very own professor of English grammar, tirelessly helped me with typing, editing, and proofreading.

The folks at Rowman & Littlefield—with special shout-outs to Tom Koerner and Carlie Wall—have been both supportive and instructive on both book projects we have worked on together.

Charles Bacall's consistent patient and expert legal counsel has long been a dependable source of wisdom for me and my colleagues.

Finally, the straw that stirs the drink: Laura Gauld, my wife. Our marital, parental, and professional journey continues . . . onward.

COLLEGES AND UNIVERSITIES

In the course of researching this book, I interviewed scores of helpful alumni, students, and parents associated with the following colleges and universities:

Beloit College (WI)
Boston University (MA)
Bowdoin College (ME)
Clark University (MA)
Colgate University (NY)
Curry College (MA)
Denison University (OH)
University of Denver (CO)
DePaul University (IL)
DePauw University (IN)
Dickinson College (PA)
Eastern Connecticut State University
Elon University (NC)
Embry-Riddle University (FL)
Emory University (GA)
Endicott College (MA)
Fashion Institute of Technology (NY)
Fordham University (NY)

Gettysburg College (PA)
Grinnell College (IA)
Harvard University (MA)
James Madison University (VA)
Juniata College (PA)
Lafayette College (PA)
Lawrence University (WI)
Lehigh University (PA)
College of Lewis & Clark (OR)
Massachusetts College of Liberal Arts
Miami-Dade Community College (FL)
Miami of Ohio University (OH)
Middlebury College (VT)
New York University (NY)
Northwestern University (IL)
University of Notre Dame (IN)
Ohio State University
Pitzer College (CA)
Providence College (RI)
Randolph-Macon College (VA)
University of Richmond (VA)
Sacred Heart University (CT)
University of South Florida
University of Southern Maine
St. Lawrence University (NY)
St. Mary's College (IN)
St. Michael's College (VT)
Springfield College (MA)
Stanford University (CA)
Southern New Hampshire University
Suffolk University (MA)
S.U.N.Y. – Stony Brook (NY)
Syracuse University (NY)
Trinity College (CT)
Tulane University (LA)
Vanderbilt University (TN)

Wheaton College (MA)

The state universities of:

Colorado
Connecticut
Maine
Maryland
Montana
New Hampshire
Texas
Vermont

BIBLIOGRAPHY

This book was also informed by the efforts of professionals and scholars dedicated to understanding and improving the human and familial condition. Risking the sin of omission, here is a short list of books you might consider for further reference.

Gauld, Laura and Gauld, Malcolm. *The Biggest Job We'll Ever Have: The Hyde School Program of Character-Based Education and Parenting*. New York: Scribner, 2002.

Gauld, M. *College Success Guaranteed: 5 Rules to Make It Happen*. Lanham, MD: Rowman & Littlefield Education, 2011.

Gottlieb, Lisa. "How to Land Your Kid in Therapy," *Atlantic Monthly* magazine. June 7, 2011.

Kindlon, Dan. *Too Much of a Good Thing: Raising Children of Character in an Indulgent Age*. New York: Hyperion, 2001.

Marano, Hana. *A Nation of Wimps: The High Cost of Invasive Parenting*. New York: Crown Archetype, 2008.

Steiner-Adair, Catherine *The Big Disconnect: Protecting Children and Family Relationships in the Digital Age*. New York: Harper Collins, 2013.

Tough, Paul. *How Children Succeed: Grit, Curiosity, and the Hidden Power of Character*. New York: Mariner Books, 2012.

Twenge, Jean. *The Narcissism Epidemic: Living in the Age of Entitlement*. New York: Free Press, 2009.

Weissbourd, Richard. *The Parents We Mean To Be: How Well-Intentioned Adults Undermine Children's Moral and Emotional Development*. New York: Mariner Books, 2010.

ABOUT THE AUTHOR

Malcolm Gauld is president of the Hyde Schools, a national community of schools—private and public—committed to helping parents help kids develop character and discover their unique potential. A graduate of Bowdoin College, he received his master's degree in education from Harvard University. Gauld is the author of *College Success Guaranteed: 5 Rules to Make It Happen* (2011). He and his wife Laura are the coauthors of *The Biggest Job We'll Ever Have*, a book intended to help parents raise children of strong character and nurture families of purpose. They and their three children live in Bath, Maine.